DEPARTMENT OF SLAVIC LANGUAGES
HAMILTON HALL, COLUMBIA UNIVERSITY
NEW YORK, NEW YORK 10027

colloquium slavicum

Beiträge zur Slavistik

Herausgeber
Heinrich Kunstmann, Universität München
Vsevolod Setchkarev, Harvard University

Band 1

jal-verlag · würzburg

To Professor Mathewson with best regards from the author.

Margaret Dalton

Andrei Siniavskii
and
Julii Daniel'

Two Soviet "Heretical" Writers

jal-verlag · würzburg
1973
ISBN 3777800821

© jal-verlag, würzburg 1973
Composed and printed by Schweinfurter Druckerei und Verlagsanstalt
Printed in Germany
ISBN 3 7778 0082 1

CONTENTS

Introduction 7

The Factual Background 10

Andrei Siniavskii (Abram Tertz): Biographical 14

Tertz's Work: 22

    1. "What Is Socialist Realism?" 22
    2. "The Trial Begins" 33
    3. "Fantastic Tales" 49

        a. "At the Circus" 50
        b. "The Graphomaniacs" 56
        c. "The Tenants" 64
        d. "You and I" 70
        e. "The Icicle" 77
        f. "Pkhents" 92

    4. *Liubimov* 98
    5. "Thoughts at Random" 128

Iulii Daniel' (Nikolai Arzhak): Biographical 138

Arzhak's Work: 141

    1. "The Hands" 141
    2. "This Is Moscow Speaking" 144
    3. "The Man from MINAP" 154
    4. "Atonement" 160

Footnotes 171

Bibliography 189

NOTE ON TRANSLITERATION

The transliteration system used here follows that presented in J. Thomas Shaw's "The Transliteration of Modern Russian for English-Language Publications" (The University of Wisconsin Press, Madison, Milwaukee, and London, 1967), System II. The only exception was made in the spelling of Tertz (instead of Terts) which seems to have become too ingrained to warrant change.

INTRODUCTION

The present study can in no way pretend to be an exhaustive treatment of two literary personalities, both of whom are still alive, relatively young, and at liberty after having served five and six year prison terms, respectively, for literary "deviation." However, it seems rather obvious that the atmosphere of relative liberalism of the late 1950's and early 60's in the Soviet Union which had produced the phenomenon of these two writers, has been superseded by a return to more rigid controls and orthodoxy. Moreover, men who have paid such a high price in terms of career, personal freedom and health, are unlikely to engage again in dangerous, clandestine ventures of their earlier years. From this point of view the "cases" of Abram Tertz and Nikolai Arzhak can be considered as closed.

There are, besides this, two points which make an analysis of the works of Tertz and Arzhak clearly worthwhile. One is the fact that, despite being exorcised by official Soviet sources, they *are* examples of Soviet Russian literature, or perhaps, of what Russian literature could be, and as such doubtlessly of interest to observers of the Soviet literary scene. Second, because of their "underground" quality, and because of the subsequent tragic fates of the two writers, these works have been heavily politicized both in East and West. In Soviet Russia, Siniavskii and Daniel' have been stamped traitors and slanderers, and thus even Siniavskii's excellent literary criticism and Daniel''s translations are doomed to oblivion. In the West, some commentators have overstressed the political aspects of Tertz's and Arzhak's writings at the expense of their literary content. It is ironical indeed, when the prosecutor of a Soviet court uses the interpretation of a "White émigré" as proof for his point![1]

For despite the political and topical elements contained in Tertz's and Arzhak's stories, it would be not only a gross over-simplification, but a mistake to term their authors political writers. In his final statement at the trial Siniavskii had made an eloquent plea for a more objective, literary approach to his work:

"... The position taken by the prosecution is as follows: *literature* (khudozhestvennaia literatura) *is a form of agitation and propaganda; agitation can be only pro-Soviet or anti-Soviet; if it is not pro-Soviet it must be anti-Soviet.* I do not agree with this ... In the depth of my soul I believe that literature cannot be approached with juridical formulas. For certainly the truth [essence] of an artistic image is complex, and often the author himself cannot explain it. I think that if Shakespeare himself were asked (I do not compare myself to Shakespeare, nobody could even think of that), if Shakespeare were asked: 'What does Hamlet mean? What does Macbeth mean? Is there no subversion?' I think Shakespeare could not give an exact answer to this. You lawyers are concerned with terms which, the more narrowly defined they are, the more precise they are. By contrast, the meaning of a literary image is the more precise, the broader it is."[2]

It is hoped that a literary interpretation of the works of Tertz and Arzhak will restore the necessary balance in a heavily distorted case.[3] In doing this I hope to render nothing but justice to Siniavskii/Tertz and Daniel'/Arzhak both as writers and people.

Since writing this Introduction certain facts on the more recent activities of Daniel'/Arzhak and Siniavskii/Tertz have become available to me through various press reports. Daniel' who is the more politically-minded of the two writers (cf. his stories "This Is Moscow Speaking," "Atonement"), showed considerable courage in camp, and consequently served his full five year term (until September, 1970). A collection of poetry, entitled "Poems from Prison" ("Stikhi iz nevoli") apparently written by him in various labor camps, has been printed in Russian by the Alexander Herzen Foundation in Amsterdam (1971). They show remarkable literary erudition, forcefulness and a genuine poetic gift. They are, however, by chronology and genre, beyond the scope of this study.

Siniavskii, whose health is reported to have suffered in labor camps, has been granted an early release (June, 1971). He is said to have written a critical essay on Pushkin, as well as a long (500 pages) literary or biographical work on his experiences and thoughts in camp under the title "A Voice from the Choir" ("Golos iz khora"). If these works exist they are so far not available.

M.D.

The Factual Background

"Literature is more important
than life."
Andrei Siniavskii[4]

No single event in recent history has reverberated through all spheres of life of a country to the extent that the death of Stalin did in Soviet Russia in 1953. A reign of terror and repression unmatched in modern times had suddenly come to an end. As the Iron Curtain which had separated Russia from the rest of the world for decades slowly began to rise, an atmosphere of hope, activity and enterprise began to be felt in all areas of life, starting with economics, and ending with arts. For literature, too, the date seemed to mark the beginning of a new period. The massive homogeneous structure of "socialist realism" — the only permissible form of literary expression for nearly 20 years — began to show cracks. Il'ia Erenburg's novel, *The Thaw (Ottepel')*, published in 1954, became synonymous with a literary re-birth. Over the years that followed Soviet writers began to gravitate toward one of the two major groupings: the dogmatists (or conservatives) — mostly officials of the Union of Soviet writers, or ideological "hack" writers — who continued to uphold the banner of socialist realism, and the revisionists (or liberals) who opposed it on artistic rather than political grounds. The latter group, large and artistically diversified, embraced both representatives of the "older" generation of writers (Il'ia Erenburg, Veniamin Kaverin, Konstantin Fedin, Alexandr Tvardovskii) and of the "younger" generation (Iurii Nagibin, Vladimir Tendriakov, Vasilii Aksenov, Iurii Kazakov, Evgenii Evtushenko, Andrei Voznesenskii, and many others). Although the stamp of approval for a literary work had to be issued, as before, according to Communist Party standards, these standards had been relaxed and the criterion of "permissibility" was getting less and less clear-cut to the censors themselves. This resulted in furious controversy and uproar in the Soviet press over works that seemed quite innocuous from the point of view of a Western observer: e.g. Vladimir Dudintsev's *Not by Bread Alone (Ne khlebom edinym)* 1956, Evgenii Evtushenko's poem "Babii Iar" 1961, Vasilii Aksenov's *Ticket to the Stars (Zvezdnyi bilet)* 1961, to name only a few. However, there were only three literary "causes célèbres" in the Soviet Union over the past 18 years that attracted world attention and concern. One was the publication in Italy of Boris Pasternak's novel *Doctor Zhivago* (1957) which earned its author the Nobel Prize for Literature abroad, but persecution and virtual silencing at home, from which Pasternak was delivered by his death in 1960. The other was the very similar Solzhenitsyn "affair," resulting from the publication of his novels *Cancer Ward (Rakovyi korpus)* 1968, and *In the First Circle (V kruge pervom)* 1969, which is still continuing. Finally, there was the case of two Soviet writers Abram Tertz and Nikolai Arzhak who had published in the West, between 1959 and 1966, a number of pseudonymous stories, among which Tertz's essay "What Is Socialist Realism?", his story, "The Trial Begins," his novel *Liubimov* (translated as *The Makepeace Experiment),* and Arzhak's tale "This Is Moscow Speaking" aroused special notice.

Early official Soviet reactions to the writings of Abram Tertz (Arzhak was not mentioned) were feigned disbelief in their authenticity, and pretended indifference: "We have little interest in the identity of the anonymous author of the article on socialist realism in the journal 'Esprit,'" said Boris Riurikov in an article entitled "Socialist Realism and Its Subverters" in 1962.[5] "Nobody is going to expose his *incognito* — he pulled on (napialil) a mask, let him go around in it." And Riurikov then proceeded to prove that the essay must be "a forgery ... fabricated in that gentlemanly-

intellectual milieu which is apparently connected with white-
émigré circles," intended to compromise the Soviet Union. Then
the press fell silent, while secret (and, no doubt, intensive) investi-
gations were initiated to uncover the identities of Tertz and Arzhak.
But it took the Soviet authorities more than 3 years before they
were successful in their search.

In October, 1965, rumors began to circulate in the West that
the Soviet scholar and literary critic Andrei Siniavskii had been
identified as Tertz and arrested in Moscow. It was further reported
that a friend of Siniavskii, a talented but hitherto little known
translator Iulii Daniel', had been arrested soon after, and charged
with having written under the name of Arzhak.[6] However, these
facts and the whole Tertz and Arzhak "affair" were not reported
in the Soviet press until about 4 months later. In January 1966, the
official silence was broken by an article in "Izvestiia" by Dmitrii
Eremin, secretary of the Moscow section of the Union of Soviet
Writers. Entitled "The Turncoats" ("Perevertyshi")[7], it attacked
the writers from a crudely political point of view, accusing them
of "vicious slander" and "anti-Soviet propaganda" which could
not be interpreted otherwise but "hostility to the Motherland."
This article was followed by other expressions of official indignation, published also in "Izvestiia," and by a lengthy discussion of
Tertz's and Arzhak's works by Zoia Kedrina, a literary critic who
was to act as an expert for the prosecution.[8] Although Kedrina's
article made the pretense of being literary, it was as unfair to Tertz
and Arzhak as was Eremin's. Calling the writers "worthy successors
of Smerdiakov [a negative personage from Dostoevskii's famous
novel *The Brothers Karamazov*] in their attempts to defile and
trample underfoot all that is human in Soviet man: friendship,
love, motherhood, family," Zoia Kedrina accused them of "real
anti-Soviet feeling," fascism, pornography, anti-Semitism and

plagiarism! Thus the "proper" atmosphere for the conviction of the writers was skillfully being prepared.

Finally, on February 10, 1966, Siniavskii and Daniel' were brought to trial in Moscow.[9] They were accused under section 1 of article 70 of the Soviet criminal code which states:

"Agitation and propaganda carried out with the purpose of subverting or weakening the Soviet regime or in order to commit particularly dangerous crimes against the state, the dissemination or production or harboring for the said purpose of literature of similar content are punishable by imprisonment for a period of from 6 months to 7 years, and with exile from 2 to 5 years." The evidence used against them were their artistic works, and the 'heretical' utterances of fictional characters which were invariably attributed to their authors as representative of their viewpoint. After 4 days of trial in which Siniavskii and Daniel' defended themselves with remarkable intelligence and courage, reversing the earlier plea of guilty (probably obtained under duress) to not guilty, they were sentenced to 7 and 5 years respectively of hard labor in camps of a "strict type".

For once, world opinion reacted with rare unanimity: innumerable protests and petitions, signed by Western writers and public figures of diverse political shadings (including Western Communist Party leaders) were addressed to the Soviet goverment. However, these protests were ignored, and Siniavskii and Daniel' disappeared behind bars. As a pendant to the Siniavskii—Daniel' case the fate of the young poet, Alexandr Gintsburg should be mentioned. After having compiled a *White Book on the Case of Andrei Siniavskii and Iulii Daniel'* (*Belaia kniga po delu A. Siniavskogo i Iu. Danielia*), which included all the material pertinent to the case, he was tried and sentenced to hard labor in January 1968.[10]

Andrei Siniavskii (Abram Tertz): Biographical

The information available on both Siniavskii and Daniel' is, for obvious reasons, rather scant. What is interesting, however, is the fact that they both are representatives of the "younger" generation of writers in the Soviet Union, i.e. those born after the 1917 Revolution, who had no personal connection with the past, and who grew up accepting (usually, unquestioningly) the political and social structure of the country. The general orthodoxy of Siniavskii's and Daniel''s backgrounds (deliberately overlooked by the prosecution at the time of their trial) makes their subsequent break, if indeed it was a break, with the ideology on which they were reared even more significant.

Andrei Siniavskii was born on October 8, 1925, in an educated Russian family in Moscow. It can be inferred that his childhood and early youth were spent in relatively comfortable circumstances, since his father, a militant revolutionary, occupied apparently a high position in the Party hierarchy. After brief participation in World War II, Siniavskii, only 19 years old at its end, turned to continuing his education. He enrolled at the philological faculty of Moscow University, where he completed his studies in 1949. In 1952 he obtained the degree of candidate (the approximate equivalent of a Ph. D.) after successfully defending a dissertation about Maxim Gor'kii's late novel, *The Life of Klim Samgin (Zhizn' Klima Samgina)*. According to the testimony of Hélène Peltier-Zamoiska, who knew Siniavskii as a student in the years 1947—50, he was a fervent patriot, an admirer of the Russian people (narod) whom he had come to know more intimately in the course of the war, a Komsomol member and convinced Communist: ". . . he could not conceive of his country having any other structure than that created in 1917. The very word 'Revolution' was for him . . . filled with the deepest meaning, holy, it portended the coming of a more just

social order, of a new humanism, called upon to renew the universe.
In the name of this belief, which was almost religious, he did not
wish to condemn the manifestations of this system, no matter how
unpleasant they appeared to him."[11] Still, Mme. Zamoiska notes,
one of their first serious debates took place "on the problem of
choice which faced Ivan Karamazov: whether it is permissible to
build a crystal palace on the corpse of a child."[12] At that time, it
seems, Siniavskii was of the opinion that "the laws of historical
development demand . . . human sacrifices."[13]

After having obtained his graduate degree, Siniavskii was
appointed lecturer of Russian literature at Moscow University,
and simultaneously senior staff member at the Gor'kii Institute of
World Literature. Two of his former (foreign) students at Moscow
University recall his helpfulness and hospitality, as well as his
"wide erudition, perspicacity, and keen artistic and literary taste"
which were "in sharp contrast to the intellectual narrowness that
was widespread at that time" (1954)[14]. Another, more personal
portrait of Siniavskii is provided by Stalin's daughter Svetlana
Allilueva, who joined the Gor'kii Institute in 1956: "He had an
impressive face with large features, which could not be called
handsome, and a big beard — a real village peasant. But there was
intelligence in his forehead, his eyes were gentle, and thought was
constantly shining on this fine, inspired face."[15] Siniavskii impressed
Allilueva by his intelligence — he was already then recognized as
"one of the most talented workers in the Section of Soviet Literature," — his eloquence, and his gentleness. Despite difficult living
conditions (at times, he dwelled in a distant, muddy village, then
in a crowded communal apartment in Moscow), Siniavskii seems to
have preserved a rare capacity for work, and a wide range of
interests. Together with his wife, a specialist in old Russian art, he
would go on excursions to the North of Russia each summer, to
photograph ancient architecture, and to collect folk art and icons.

Allilueva felt in him an "inborn, pure, poetical religiousness" which was combined with a "sharp critical mind, which mercilessly analyzed everything — the craft of the poet, the nuances of the word, and his own feelings and experiences."[16] The wide range of Siniavskii's knowledge and interests is also evidenced by his numerous essays, books and reviews.

His first publication seems to have been an article on Maiakovskii's aesthetics ("Ob estetike Maiakovskogo"), which was part of his thesis for a diploma (diplomnaia rabota), entitled "The Aesthetic Positions of Maiakovskii" ("Esteticheskie pozitsii Maiakovskogo").[17] This was followed by articles on Gor'kii, Bagritskii, and on early and recent Soviet literature in various publications of the Academy of Sciences and of the Institute of World Literature.[18] Together with the literary historian A.N. Menshutin, Siniavskii collaborated on an anthology of recent Soviet poetry *(Den' russkoi poezii)*, 1958.[19] One of his most important scholarly contributions was a book on the poetry of the first years of the Revolution *(Poeziia pervykh let revoliutsii, 1917—20)*, written also in collaboration with A.N. Menshutin. Published in 1964, in a small edition (4,000 copies), this book will doubtlessly become a rarity. Having known and admired Pasternak, Siniavskii contributed to his *post-mortem* "rehabilitation" by writing an introduction to a more complete edition of Pasternak's poetry.[20] The fact that Siniavskii's interests were not confined only to literature is attested by his collaboration on a book about Picasso with the art historian I.N. Golomshtok, which appeared in 1960.[21] At the time of his arrest Siniavskii was writing an essay on Old Russian art which was to be entitled "The Land and Sky of Old Russia" ("Zemlia i nebo drevnei Rusi").[22]

As a literary critic Siniavskii was associated with the liberal journal "Novyi Mir," which printed his reviews on various poets and writers, such as Anatolii Safronov (August 1959), Ol'ga

Berggol'ts (May 1960), Boris Pasternak (March 1962), Robert Frost (January 1964), Ivan Shevtsov (December 1964), Evgenii Dolmatovskii (March 1965), and Evgenii Evtushenko.[23] Siniavskii seems to have also written on Akhmatova, Khlebnikov, Babel', and perhaps some other not quite "acceptable" poets and writers.[24]

The internal ideological evolution which eventually led Siniavskii to "Abram Tertz"[25] is, of course, impossible to trace. Perhaps an element of youthful ferment and dissatisfaction with the obvious discrepancy between the Communist ideal and reality had been present quite early.[26] No doubt the arrest of his "orthodox" father who fell victim to one of Stalin's last purges in 1951, must have dealt a serious jolt to Andrei Siniavskii's faith in the justice of the system. This was followed by the death of Stalin and the revelation of Stalin's crimes at the 20th Party Congress of the Communist Party of the Soviet Union in 1956, which shattered yesterday's "god," and deprived many "believers" of their ideological base. This general feeling is well expressed by Siniavskii (Tertz) in his essay on socialist realism:

"The death of Stalin inflicted an irreparable loss upon our religious aesthetic system, and it is difficult to make up for it by the newly revived cult of Lenin. Lenin is too much like an ordinary man (chelovekopodoben), too realistic by his very nature, small of stature, a civilian. Stalin, on the other hand, was specifically created for the hyperbole that awaited him. Mysterious, allseeing, almighty, he was the living monument of our epoch, and lacked only one quality in order to become god — immortality."[27]

As a scholar too Siniavskii must have become early aware of the limitations which Communist ideology places on any serious and objective research. He had no choice but to be "orthodox," with just a touch of a deviation into aesthetics. Thus in his earliest article on Maiakovskii (written in 1949), he dutifully quotes Lenin and Stalin (the latter being still alive at that time), and seems to voice full agreement with Maiakovskii's theory of the primacy of life, i.e. reality, specifically political reality, over art. Yet Siniavskii's private remark to Mme. Peltier-Zamoiska to the effect that literature is more important than life (cf. epigraph) made in that same year, appears retrospectively not only like a tragic foreshadowing of his own fate, but also as a conscious polemic with Maiakovskii, on whom he was just working.

It is unfortunately impossible to assess Siniavskii's scholarly contributions in the anonymous "Histories" of the Academy of Sciences. It is similarly difficult to extract his point of view from the collective work with Menshutin. Still, his authorial presence seems to be felt in the general tone of the book: in the detached, scholarly evaluation of that turbulent period, in the attempts to separate bad poetry from good, no matter what its revolutionary ardor, and in the relatively objective treatment of such controversial figures as Marina Tsvetaeva, Sergei Esenin, Nikolai Gumilev, and Anna Akhmatova.

More insight into Siniavskii's literary approach is provided by his essays on Maiakovskii, and especially on Gor'kii, where he tended to concentrate on problems of form and structure rather than political ideology. Thus in analyzing Gor'kii's late novel *The Life of Klim Samgin*, often dismissed as a weak, unwieldy piece of writing, Siniavskii discovers in it "an amazing... internal cohesiveness" and unity.[28] This, he points out, is the result of such devices as "mirror-like" (zerkal'noe) composition (various characters reflecting one or another moral or psychological quality of the hero who forms the focal point in the novel), historical periodization and continuity (characters epitomizing certain historical periods, and appearing or disappearing from the novel in historical sequence), certain leitmotifs (e.g. the singing of the song "Dubinushka" at various periods in the hero's life), characterization through set phrases, aphorisms, etc. Similarly, in discussing Gor'kii's satire, Siniavskii points to the literary heritage of Saltykov-Shchedrin in Gor'kii, and ends up by finding parallels between Gor'kii and Maiakovskii in their satirical devices.

Maiakovskii and Gor'kii, the two pillars of socialist realism, occupy an important position in Siniavskii's literary studies. And if he rejected them both later on — theoretically (in his essay on socialist realism) and practically (in his own works), the former still with a touch of admiration for his psychological and artistic "wholeness," the latter with scorn for his naive pretentiousness — it was after a very thorough and careful examination. It is probably because of this immersion into the works of Maiakovskii and Gor'kii that there are occasionally even faint echoes of these two writers in Tertz's own works: daring metaphors suggestive of Maiakovskii (cf. "The Trial Begins"), elements of Gor'kii's "polyphony,"[29] and strong political satire, which becomes especially clearly revealed in the novel *Liubimov*. It is perhaps also not quite accidental that the name of its hero, Tikhomirov, is a name quoted several times in Gor'kii's letters.[30]

Siniavskii's acute aesthetic taste is especially noticeable in his various reviews of poetry. He was quick to react to the genuine, original and to reject poetic mediocrity and imitativeness. Thus discussing Ol'ga Berggol'ts, he calls her poems "the most tragic" in contemporary poetry, filled with "moral purity" and the idea of "unity of the personal and universal."[31] He was intrigued by a new translation of Robert Frost's poetry, and by Frost's "aesthetic program" of "building bridges from one human being to another."[32] Evgenii Dolmatovskii's poems, on the other hand, are dismissed as "warm" (rather than "hot" or "cold") and uninteresting. Siniavskii pointed to Anatolii Safronov's obvious imitations of Maiakovskii, the author being "a captive of his own phraseology."[33] He was critical of Evtushenko's "modernism" (obvious borrowings from Blok, Esenin, Maiakovskii), and his inability to reach a poetic

stature of his own. One of the best tributes to Siniavskii as a critic
of poetry is a letter by Pasternak, written before the *Doctor
Zhivago* "affair," in which the latter thanks Siniavskii for an
article devoted to an analysis of his poetry:

"Dear Andrei Donatovich,

I thank you from all my heart for the joy which you gave me.
Irrespective of the fact to whom it was devoted, it was a great
pleasure to read an essay which expressed with such exhaustive
conciseness the essence of the [poet] analyzed, his "soul", and
"philosophy", and which was written with such natural elegance,
reminiscent of the best memories of my youth — such as Aksakov's
biography of Tiutchev, or Strakhov's articles on Fet.

With what fortuitous completeness you understood all the
main things in me! And how limpidly, harmoniously you ex-
pounded, developed and explained it to the end, without leaving
anything out! ..... Once more, I thank you for your work, for
your desire for good which is felt in it, for your freely breathing
thought, for the unhurried, modest and dignified tone of your
article, for your ability to overcome lucidly all the sham and the
superfluous.

Yours, Boris Pasternak" (dated June 29, 1957)[34]

Siniavskii's scholarly career could not have been very easy. He
did not join the Communist Party despite earlier membership in the
Komsomol, which must have been a serious drawback for advancement. He probably made enemies among the more "orthodox"
writers by some of his reviews. Many of his essays and articles
remained unpublished for years, as he testified at the trial. It was
perhaps partly due to his frustrations as a scholar, partly because of
his desire for creative writing that "Abram Tertz" was born. The
first story, "At the Circus," which came to be included later on in
his collection of "Fantastic Tales" was written already in 1955.

This was followed, in 1958, by the essay "What Is Socialist Realism?" (first published anonymously in the French journal "Esprit" in Paris in February 1959), and the story "The Trial Begins" (also published in 1959). The other stories that make up the "Fantastic Tales" were written in 1959 ("You and I," "The Tenants"), 1960 ("Graphomaniacs"), and 1961 ("The Icicle"), and appeared collectively in Paris in 1961. A novel *Liubimov*, written in 1961—62, appeared in 1964—65 under the English title *The Makepeace Experiment*. A collection of thoughts and aphorisms, written over a period of several years and entitled "Thoughts at Random" were published in 1965. After the arrest of Siniavskii in September 1965, a last story, "Pkhents" reached the West; it was published in the English journal "Encounter" in March 1966. Thus seven stories, a novel, an essay, and a collection of thoughts are the literary heritage of Abram Tertz.

Tertz's Work

1. "What Is Socialist Realism?"[35] ("Chto takoe sotsialisticheskii realizm?"), 1958

Tertz's first published work, written in the aftermath of the 20th Party Congress, was an essay devoted to an analysis of socialist realism, the only "authorized" method of Soviet literature, which had dominated the literary scene since the early 30's. The importance of this essay, both in terms of Soviet literature in general, and Tertz in particular, cannot be sufficiently stressed. For this was the first bold and free inquiry into a literary-political dogma that had hitherto been considered untouchable. As far as Tertz himself was concerned, the essay laid the theoretical groundwork for his subsequent artistic work by defining his position vis à vis socialist realism, and by giving his own artistic credo. Finally, it also reflected well Tertz's remarkable literary erudition, his passionate, paradoxical temperament, and provided an excellent example of the brilliancy of his style.

The essay is divided into 3 parts. The first, and probably the most challenging and interesting, makes an analysis of the "aesthetic and psychological premises" which underlie the phenomenon of socialist realism. The second part is a comparison of socialist realist literature with Russian 19th century literature. The third part connects socialist realism with 18th century classicism, and makes some prognoses on its future.

Tertz's definition of the first part is (probably intentionally) a misnomer. It is primarily an analysis of the ideological premises (Communism) which underlie socialist realism, and of Tertz's own "heretical" views upon them. The aesthetic and psychological aspects issue from the ideological base and are, in a sense, secondary to it. But it probably seemed safer to Tertz to pretend to be speaking about aesthetics and psychology rather than about Communism and Marxism. The most distinctive and important feature of Communism, according to Tertz, is its teleological, purpose-oriented character, its goal being the eventual triumph and realization of Communist theories. A tendency toward purposeful action and thought is basic to human nature, says Tertz, as a reaction to the chaos and apparent indifference of the universe. It manifests itself on the concrete, physical level ("I stretch out my hand in order to get some coins"), as well as on the abstract, intellectual ("I write a novel in order to become famous and to earn the gratitude of posterity"). The whole history of mankind, in Tertz's view, is a succession of various Purposes: Christianity ("Purpose in its most elusive form"), Individualism (Renaissance, Humanism, Democracy), and finally, Communism. Tertz sees definite parallels between Christianity and Communism: both manifest a rigid weltanschauung, fervent idealism and intolerance. Yet the greater appeal and strenght of Communism vis à vis Christianity lies, according to Tertz, in its "this-worldliness," and the promise of a paradise on earth.

Communist teleology pervades and dominates all spheres of life from technology to art. In the area of aesthetics it has produced socialist realist art, "the most purposeful art of our time," which has only one purpose — the portrayal and glorification of the Communist Purpose. And while this may create some psychological problems for an outsider, to a Communist "believer" the question of "freedom" of creativity does not arise. For, asks Tertz: "What freedom, permit me to say, can the religious person demand of his God? The freedom to praise Him even more ardently?"[36]

The irony of the matter, in Tertz's view is, however, that ideals cannot be implemented in practice; even worse, they have a tendency of turning into their exact opposites. This, Tertz finds, has happened to Communism which has not built its promised paradise on earth, but has returned to many of the features and practices of its predecessor and ideological enemy (Czarism). This has also happened to socialist realist literature which has produced nothing but boring uniformity.

Tertz then proceeds to a detailed discussion of socialist realist literature (part 2). The idea of Purpose, which underlies socialist realist novels, determines their tone, subject matter and characterization. The tone is, obviously, optimistic. By a clever juxtaposition of titles of well-known Western and Soviet novels Tertz demonstrates the "minor" tone of the former (e.g. *Death in the Afternoon, To Whom the Bell Tolls*) versus the "major" tone of the latter (e.g. *Happiness, First Joys, The Victors*). Most socialist realist novels furthermore have happy endings in terms of the idea of Purpose which must be ultimately victorious (even if their respective heroes or heroines perish in the course of action). The subject of socialist realist novels too, whether they be taken from the realms of the present, the past, or human psychology, invariably emphasize the progress of Purpose. But the cornerstone of socialist realism, and simultaneously the element which distinguishes it most strikingly from earlier Russian literature is, according to Tertz, the positive hero. The positive hero is not simply a good man, but "a hero illuminated by the light of the most ideal ideal, an example worthy of all possible imitation, 'a man-mountain from whose peak the future can be seen'".[37] In terms of Russian literature of the 19th century, the positive hero is a complete break with tradition. For the 19th century did not have positive heroes, just as it did not have the faith on which they grow. The 19th century was "tolerant, atheistic, disoriented," while most of the great writers of that period from Dostoevskii and Tolstoi to Merezhkovskii were "God-seekers" precisely because they did not have a God. Tertz sees an interesting parallel to the 19th century's "godlessness" and striving for an unattainable Purpose in the plot of the first great Russian novel in verse, Pushkin's *Eugene Onegin,* with its twice-rejected-love story. All Russian literary heroines, starting with Pushkin's Tatiana and ending with Blok's "Beautiful Lady," seem to Tertz to embody the ideal, the Purpose, which the heroes, "superfluous men" cannot reach. For the landmark of the 19th century was the superfluous man — the man without, or beyond Purpose. The end of the superfluous man was heralded at the beginning of the 20th century by the appearance of the positive hero in the works of Gorkii and Blok. By the 1920's, the superfluous man, the hero of 19th century Russian literature, had been eliminated: he either turned into a negative character, or transformed himself duly into a positive character.

It is not the 19th century, but rather the 18th century with its "idea of political purposefulness, feeling of superiority, and clear consciousness that 'God is with us'"[38] which is akin to socialist realism, says Tertz (part 3). Tertz cites the odes of Derzhavin, court poet of Catherine the Great, as typical examples of 18th century literature. The subtitle of one of Derzhavin's poems says "a picture of what a great lord ought to be." The same subtitle, Tertz claims, could be applied to socialist realism, for it too represents the world and man as they *ought* to be, not as they *are.* Socialist realism proceeds from an ideal image to which living reality is adapted. The socialist realist formula which demands that life be depicted "truthfully in its revolutionary development" means nothing else but the portrayal of things as they should be, and not as they are. And thus socialist realism should really be called socialist classicism. For besides ideology, it contains also some other features of classicism: solemnity, pathos, high style. While "the first heroes of Soviet literature stormed the capitalist strongholds with torn bast shoes on their feet and vulgar oaths on their lips,"[39] in subsequent "socialist classicist" novels they have

acquired comeliness, and refinement in their clothes and manners."[40]

Tertz traces the development of "socialist classicism" through
a short period of revolutionary romanticism (its outstanding
representative being Maiakovskii) to the present. Over the years
the level of Soviet literature has steadily deteriorated, finds Tertz.
But this, he says, is not so much the fault of socialist realism, as
the fault of Soviet writers who try to combine features which
cannot be combined: elements of 19th century realism (such as
psychological analysis of characters, prosaic description of *byt*,[41]
truthful depiction of life), and the demands of a "classical,"
"religious" art (such as allegory, high declamatory style, an elevated
ideal). The result of such a mixture is "neither classicism nor
realism," but a "semi-classical semi-art of a non-too-socialist non-
realism."[42] At the beginning of his essay Tertz had posed an apparently paradoxical question as to the actual existence of socialist
realism. For, he had argued, can there be a "socialist, capitalist,
Christian, or Mohammedan realism?" Now, after having analyzed
its ideological and historical origins and development, he comes to
the following conclusions: 1. Real socialist realism, while in theory
possible, is not practiced in the Soviet Union, and 2. What present-
day Soviet writers mean by socialist realism is not socialist realism
at all, but a contradiction in terms. Because Tertz has little faith
in a revival of socialist realism (the necessary "faith" is missing
since the death of Stalin), he suggests an interim solution to fill the
existing literary vacuum, which is simultaneously his own artistic
credo:

"Right now I put my hope in an art that is phantasmagoric,
with hypotheses instead of a Purpose, an art in which the grotesque will replace realistic descriptions. Such an art would corres-
pond best to the spirit of our time. May the exaggerated imagery
of Hoffmann, Dostoevskii, Goya, Chagall and Maiakovskii (the

most socialist realist of all), and of many other realists and non-realists teach us how to be truthful with the help of absurd fantasy.

While losing our faith, we have not lost our enthusiasm about the metamorphoses of god that take place before our eyes, before the enormous peristalsis of his entrails — the convolutions of his brain. We do not know where to go; but realizing that there is nothing to be done about it, we begin to think, to make conjectures and assumptions. Perhaps we will devise something marvelous. But it will no longer be socialist realism."[43]

Although to "orthodox" Soviet literary critics Tertz's essay is heresy by definition, its general style is not new in the context of earlier Russian literature. For it follows the tradition of Russian 19th century polemical writings which had combined literary criticism with critique of social conditions, or with exposition of radical ideas — one of the bestknown examples of this kind being Dobroliubov's sociological analysis of Goncharov's famous novel *Oblomov,* entitled "What Is 'Oblomovism'?" ("Chto takoe 'Oblomovshchina'?"). More specifically, Tertz's essay seems to echo the title and even certain ideas from Tolstoi's controversial discourse on art "What Is Art?" ("Chto takoe iskusstvo?") published in 1897—98. Tolstoi's repudiation of the traditional (metaphysical and aesthetic) criteria of art, his search for a new all-embracing definition of art, his highly subjective historical perspective, all these elements have some parallels in Tertz's rejection of socialist realism, his plea for a new phantasmagoric art, and his vision of history as a succession of Purposes. Moreover, Tolstoi's concept of true art as religious art, and true literature as "literature with a purpose" are brilliantly reworked in Tertz's essay in Marxian terms.[44] Even Tertz's method of analyzing socialist realism is, at times, reminiscent of the Tolstoian "estrangement" (ostranenie), as e.g. when he takes it out of its political, Marxian context.

Tertz raises two main issues in his essay, a literary and a political-philosophical one, namely on the essence and validity of
both socialist realism and communism. In terms of the literary
problem,[45] he finds that socialist realism is, theoretically at least,
perfectly acceptable as the expression of a "religious" art, based
on a "religious" ideology. For art can be "narrowly religious,
dumbly governmental, devoid of individuality, and yet great,"[46]
he says, citing the examples of ancient Egyptian art and of Russian iconography. It is simply because the ideological basis for
such art is missing in Russia — the Stalin cult was the closest to
creating it — that he advocates the renunciation of socialist realism, and the search for new art forms. Tertz's ironic treatment
of the positive hero (who does not tire "to speak about Communism at work, and at home, while visiting friends or taking a
walk, on his deathbed and on the bed of love"),[47] and of the dull
socialist realist novels on industrial and agricultural achievements
(in which "the reader gradually finds out how, despite all break-
downs, a machine was put to work, or how the collective farm
'Victory', despite rainy weather, collected a rich harvest of
corn . . .")[48] fit, of course into his theoretical rejection of current
socialist realist novels: they are examples of a contamination of
styles, of classicism and realism, which result in nothing but an
"atrocious literary salad." But there can be no doubt that Tertz
is also voicing his own personal, artistic disapproval of the cru-
deness and didacticism of Soviet literary production, and that the
feels much like Chekhov "who feared pretentiousness worse than
fire" and who "frowned with embarrassment" when he first en-
countered the loud proclamations of Gor'kii's positive hero (in
the novel *The Petty Bourgeois/ Meshchane*). Tertz's sympathies lie
clearly with the "ironic, disoriented, atheistic" 19th century, and
he seems to identify himself with Lermontov's Demon who
wanted "to become reconciled with heaven ... to love ... to

pray ... to believe in the good."[49] It is Tertz's lack of "faith" which prevents him from being a true socialist realist (as Maiakovskii, in his opinion, was). And this lack of faith leads to the second issue which underlies Tertz's essay and which is philosophical rather than literary.

Tertz's discussion of Communism is (perhaps partly, intentionally) more ambiguous and less clear-cut than had been his analysis of socialist realism. It is also charged with much more personal emotion and involvement than the literary discussion. Tertz raises a series of questions: on the validity of Communism in absolute terms, on the discrepancy between ideal and practice, on the eternal problem of ends and means. There is a Dostoevskian tenor to these questions not only in terms of ideas but also of style — vehement, paradoxical, ironic, pathetic — suggestive of a modern "man from unterground." The Dostoevskian element is further enhanced by Tertz's Slavophile feelings, his rejection of such Western concepts as democracy (which he distrusts), and individualism (which, in his opinion, produces a "humanistic" egotism interested only in personal salvation).

Tertz takes issue with Marxism's claim of being the final step in the development of mankind. With profound irony he paraphrases Marx's "brilliant discovery" — a simplified vision of history: "At once everything fell into place. Iron necessity, a strict hierarchical order fettered the stream of centuries. The ape, getting up on its hind legs, began its triumphant procession toward Communism. The system of the primitive commune is necessary in order to develop the system of slavery; slavery is necessary in order to bring forth feudalism; feudalism is necessary for us to create capitalism; and capitalism in its turn is necessary in order to give birth to Communism. That is all. The beautiful goal has been reached, the pyramid is crowned, history is at an end."[50]

Tertz does not believe in Marxism as the final Purpose.

Rather, he views it, in Hegelian terms, as just another Purpose which will eventually be superseded by something else: "... after many centuries a Purpose will rise above the world, the name of which nobody knows yet ..."[51]. Perhaps too, there is in this an echo of Dostoevskii who believed that humanity prefers the process of striving to the goal achieved: "And who knows (it is impossible to be absolutely sure about it), perhaps the whole aim mankind is striving to achieve on earth merely lies in this incessant process of achievement, or (to put it differently) in life itself, and not really in the attainment of any goal, which, needles to say, can be nothing else but twice-two-makes-four, that is to say, a formula; but twice-two-makes-four it not life, gentlemen. It is the beginning of death."[52] The question of striving (= life) versus Purpose achieved (= death) as Zamiatin formulated it (in his famous essay, "O literature, revoliutsii, entropii, i o prochem," 1923), seems also to be reflected in Tertz's love for the Russian Revolution which is accorded the highest place in his scale of emotional values. "Unlike the Party, the state, the Ministry of State Security (MGB), collectivization, Stalin, the Revolution does not need justification by a Communist paradise that awaits us. It is justified by itself, emotionally, like love, like inspiration. And although the Revolution was carried out in the name of Communism, its own name is not less sweet for us. Perhaps, even more sweet ..."[53]

    As to the cause of the Revolution, the Communist "religion" itself, Tertz's attitude toward it is much less positive. It seems to be close to that of an "intelligent, cultured Roman patrician" versus rising Christianity, i.e. he could not bring forth arguments against its ideals, even if he could not share its faith, and disapproved of its practices: "Could he [the Roman patrician] say that God conceived as Love and Goodness is bad, low, ugly? And can we say that universal happiness, promised in the Communist future is bad?"[54] But what is this vision of a Communist paradise, fashioned after the idea of the Christian paradise, if not a series of negations of materialistic concepts? "Words fail us when we want to tell about Communism. We choke from enthusiasm, and in order to convey the splendor which awaits us, we make use of negative comparisons, primarily. There, under Communism, there will be no rich and no poor, no money, no wars, no prisons, no frontiers, no illnesses, and perhaps even no death. There, everyone will eat as much as he wants, and work as much as he wants, and labor instead of suffering will bring only joy. As Lenin promised, we'll make toilets of pure gold . . ."[55]

If the future looks like a parody of the Christian paradise, the present is likewise uninspiring. For the results of the implementation of Communist ideology are a terrifying uniformity and conformity of thought in man that exceed anything that any other "religion" was able to achieve: "Yes, indeed, we outdo other periods and peoples in regard to uniformity [of thought], we resemble each other and are not ashamed of this resemblance, and those who suffer from superfluous difference of thought, we punish severely, removing them from life and literature. In a country, where even anti-Party elements confess their mistakes and want to improve as soon as possible, where even incorrigible enemies of the people request to be shot, there can be no substantial difference of thought . . ."[56] It seems that under those circumstances the day is not far when, as Dostoevskii foresaw it, man would be nothing but "a piano key or an organ punch," and when all human acts would be "calculated according to laws, mathematically, like the table of logarythms, up to 108.000," and would be "entered into a calendar."[57]

The terrible discrepancy between ideal and practice, between the Communist ideal and the actual result, is what Tertz deplores most. The passage in which he speaks about it, is one of the strongest in the whole essay in terms of its emotional impact, and its undoubted sincerity. It is, however, not so much an indictment of

Communism, as an anguished outcry against the impossibility of realizing ideals, a reiteration of the words of Dostoevskii's character Shigalev who said: "Starting with unlimited freedom, I end up with unlimited despotism".[58]

"So that prisons would vanish for ever, we built new prisons. So that frontiers between states should fall, we surrounded ourselves with a Chinese wall. So that work, in the future, would become rest and pleasure, we introduced forced labor. So that not a single drop of blood be shed any more, we killed, and killed and killed.

In the name of the Purpose we had to sacrifice all that we had in reserve, and to use the same means which our enemies used — to glorify Imperial Russia, to write lies in "Pravda" ["Truth"], to put a Czar on the now empty throne, to introduce officers' epaulettes and torture ... sometimes it seemed that only one final sacrifice was needed for the complete triumph of Communism — the renunciation of Communism."[59]

Tertz feels this discrepancy so keenly because it is such a terrible let-down after the Russian Revolution, *his* revolution. But it is precisely here, where Tertz's answer to the question of "ends and means" takes on an unexpected turn. When Ivan Karamazov asked Alesha whether he would agree to build human happiness on the unavenged tears of a little child, Alesha (and Dostoevskii) recoiled in horror.[60] But Tertz, despite his previous passionate outburst against the Communist "results" seems to accept them as inevitable. For he finds that "achievements are never identical with the original aim." And just as the abuses of Christianity (the Inquisition, the massacre of St. Bartholomew's night) still add up to "one great Christian culture," thus Communism, despite its many deficiences, has still some resemblance to its original idea.

This seemingly paradoxical and strangely conciliatory deduction, however, reflects Tertz's position quite well. He lacks the ideological "purity" of Dostoevskii's "man from underground" who could wholeheartedly denounce the evils of utilitarianism and utopian socialism, because deep down in his soul he had a counterbalance that he could juxtapose to them: faith in Christ. Tertz, a modern man, has no such faith at this point, and is incapable therefore of rejecting his whole ideological background. Perhaps he can be accused of lack of consistency, and certain pragmatism. But in his mistrust of Western ideas, there is no other way out for him, exept the Russian way, the path of 1917. Being pushed by the past (the Revolution) and pulled forward by the future (Communism), Tertz finds himself psychologically caught in a squeeze from which there is no escape. For "behind us and ahead of us rise sanctuaries too splendid to make us dare to rise against them."[61]

At his trial Siniavskii had said that his essay was written from an idealistic, rather than Marxist or socialist realist point of view. But in the final analysis, Tertz's rebellion remains *within* Communism, not *without* it. He has no system to oppose it, no faith to counter it. Perhaps he did not intend to give ready answers to the questions which he posed in his essay. Perhaps, all he wanted to do, not only in aesthetic, but also in philosophical terms, was to start "thinking, making conjectures, surmises." And in this he certainly succeeded.

2. "The Trial Begins" ("Sud idet"), 1958[62]

"The Trial Begins," Tertz's first story to appear in print, is in some ways his most complex, most deliberately written tale, and a good example of the "many-layeredness" of Tertz's fiction. On one level it is time-bound, realistic, political. This was how the Soviet court chose to interpret it at Siniavskii's own trial.[63] On a deeper level, it is philosophical and symbolic. Many of Tertz's ideas on Marxism and Communism which he had expressed in his

essay on socialist realism are repeated in the story, which is a kind
of fictional "pendant" to it. In this combination of theoretical
ideas and fiction lie both the strength and the weakness of "The
Trial Begins": while it has strong ideological impact and weight,
the theories, at times, stick out and are too obvious. In *Liubimov*,
his other political-philosophical tale, Tertz was more subtle in
integrating his theories into the fictional material. But even if
Liubimov may be termed better fiction, "The Trial Begins" is a
more provocative and forceful piece of writing.

The title of the story (as the story itself) refers to the trial and
sentencing of a group of prominent Jewish physicians for allegedly
conspiring to poison Stalin during the last months of his life
(1952-53). And although Tertz does not present that trial, the fate
of the Jewish doctor Rabinovich, prosecuted for performing illegal
abortions (as part of this alleged conspiracy) seems to illustrate the
absurdity and arbitrariness of the whole Jewish doctors' "case."
The sentencing of two other characters — Serezha Globov for
"heretical" thoughts and the anonymous narrator for "heretical"
writing — further serve to emphasize the atmosphere of trials. But
there is felt, beyond these concrete "cases," the presence of a larger,
mysterious, Kafkaesque Judgment in the story. "The trial goes on,
the trial goes on in all the world," says the narrator in one of his
asides. "And it is no longer Rabinovich, exposed by the City
Prosecutor, but all of us, no matter how many, who are taken to
trial and questioning every day, every night. And this is called
history."[64] Thus reality reaches into the realm of the metaphysical,
into the problems of individual guilt, individual responsibility
versus history.

The story, presented by the anonymous narrator (who remains
in the background throughout the main action), consists of a
prologue, 7 short chapters and an epilogue, and takes place in
Moscow between September 1952 and March 1953.[65] On the more

obvious, "realistic" level, it may be said to be a re-working of the "fathers and sons" theme, a Soviet *Petersburg*[66], in which outside events are reflected or refracted through the main characters of the story: the Public Prosecutor, Vladimir Petrovich Globov, his young, idealistic son (by his first wife) Serezha, and Globov's beautiful, immoral (second) wife, Marina. A love plot connects Marina with the lawyer Karlinskii, and a "political" plot connects Serezha and his school-mate Katia on one hand, and Globov and Rabinovich on the other. Beyond this, "The Trial Begins" is also an ironic commentary on the life of the Soviet bureaucratic élite with its "bourgeois" values, and its hypocrisy, and a vivid portrayal of the atmosphere of repression and control during the last days of Stalin. There are some marvellous ironic descriptions of *byt* and characters, e.g. Marina's birthday party (chapter 1) with its atmosphere of decadent eroticism; the party of the interrogators (chapter 6), at which the political vigilance of the participants increases proportionately to the amount of liquor consumed; the figure of the interrogator with the misleading name of Skromnykh (Modest) and his gentle hobby of embroidering between interrogation sessions etc. The two plainclothesmen, Tolia and Vitia who turn up through the story (e.g. in the same café where Marina and Karlinskii meet, in the zoo where Katia and Serezha promenade), are not only illustrative of the everwatchful eye of the Leader, but also of the "idealism" that such a profession may engender. All their thoughts are directed to improving on the methods of control over the human mind: thus Tolia wants to invent a dragnet that would catch up all writings that are thrown into the sewage pipes, while Vitia, an avid reader of Herbert Wells, dreams of an apparatus, a "thoughtscope," which would check automatically, at any time and any distance even those who are silent, and do not write. This is how he visualizes the future application of his machine:

"Good morning, citizen. What was it that you were thinking about four minutes seventeen seconds ago? We know everything. If you do not believe it, we can show you the film." And the citizen thus confronted, immediately confesses: "I can't deny it — I am guilty. I am a contemptible hireling of a certain foreign power. Ever since my childhood I am concerned with the restoration of capitalism and the filing away of railroad bridges . . ."[67]

On a deeper level it becomes obvious that Tertz is using the "fathers and sons" theme to express his theory of Purpose, in both historical and psychological terms. A graphic illustration of the rise, growth, and inevitable decay of historical Purposes is given during the encounter between Globov and Rabinovich in chapter 4. As regards personal Purposes, Tertz had suggested in his essay that man needs a Purpose in order to exist, for he is afraid of "purposeless" freedom. This idea is poignantly expressed by the narrator in the story at the moment of Stalin's death (the collapse of the Communist Purpose for many "believers") by comparing "purposeless" man to a stray dog (chapter 7): "The Master had died. Everything became empty. One felt like sitting down, and raising one's head toward the sky, howling like homeless dogs do. The dogs who have lost their masters stray throughout the earth and sniff the air in anguish . . . Seeing a human being they run to the side and look for a long time — isn't it *he?* — but they don't come near. They wait, they always wait, and beg someone with their long glance. 'O come! Feed us! Beat us as much as you wish (not too hard, please). But only come . . . Wough! I do not want freedom. I need a Master!'"[68] All the major characters in the story are in search (or in possession) of Purpose, even though these purposes vary greatly. And while being characters in their own rights, they are also to some degree symbolic of these purposes.

The "hero" of the story, Vladimir Petrovich Globov, who has risen from an obscure peasant background to the position of Public

Prosecutor, represents the "fathers" and is simultaneously ideologically the most "pure" character in the story. He has an unshakable faith in the Communist Purpose, no matter how it may manifest itself, and is ready to sacrifice everything to it — even his only son Serezha. "The goal justifies the means" is his credo. The parallel between the Communist and the Christian faith, which Tertz had pointed out in the essay, is most poignantly evident through him. In a dream-like sequence Globov sees Serezha being put to trial (before it actually happens), and denounces him and himself in reversed Gospel terms: "With your beautiful means one can only perish, but we must win, win by all means. So judge him, citizen prosecutor, if you consider it necessary. Judge me with him too, for having been soft. It is better if tens and hundreds of innocent people suffer than that one enemy is saved."[69] In the course of the action of the story Globov's family life (which, paradoxically, he cherishes greatly) collapses: his wife Marina deprives him of a much-wanted child by having an abortion (it remains intentionally unclear whether Rabinovich is involved in it or not), since she does not want to spoil her beauty. His son Serezha becomes involved in a childish "conspiracy," and is tried and exiled to Siberia. Ekaterina Petrovna, his mother-in-law by his first wife, and a close friend and fellow-Communist, turns from him when he allows Serezha to be sentenced. But although Globov suffers deeply, his faith in the Communist Purpose sustains him. After getting drunk in his study and engaging in a violent battle with an imaginary enemy (during which he hacks most of his furniture into pieces), Globov addresses himself to the bust of Stalin: "Master! The enemy is fleeing! They have killed my daughter, have stolen my son. My wife has betrayed me, and my mother renounced me. But I stand before you, wounded, left by all, and I say: 'The Purpose has been reached! We have conquered! Do you hear, Master — we have conquered. Do you hear me?'"[70]

Globov's vigilance in the service of Communism leads him to
uncover the doctors' "conspiracy" through the case of doctor
Rabinovich: "From illegal abortion it is one step to murder, and
from there it's not far to more serious subversion," he says.[71] For
at the base of the case lies an ideologically (rather than nationally)
colored anti-Semitism, i.e. distrust of Jews as representatives of
independant, non-conformist thought (cf. "At the Circus"): "... He
had already prosecuted some Rabinovich previously, perhaps even
two or three of them. Can one remember them all? The fact that
they were hostile to socialism by virtue of their petty-bourgeois
nature was clear to every schoolboy nowadays. Of course, there
were exceptions. Il'ia Erenburg. But on the other hand — Trotskii,
Radek, Zinov'ev, Kamenev, critics-cosmopolitans ... A certain
inborn tendency toward treason ..."[72] And while Globov stamps
Rabinovich a "child murderer," he himself becomes, ironically, a
child-murderer when Katia is trampled to death in a stampede at
Stalin's funeral. The death of his master Stalin is the greatest blow
to Globov's faith, for to him Stalin must have appeared nearly
immortal. But he survives the crisis, and in the epilogue it is learned
that he prospers under the new leadership.

The "sons," represented by Serezha Globov (and, peripherally,
by his school friend, Katia), can no longer believe in the Purpose of
their fathers, and rebel against it. Serezha sees clearly the dichotomy
between ideal and practice, the subjectivity of the Communist point
of view, and in consequence he searches for a Purpose. In a conversation with his father about "just and unjust wars" (chapter 1)
Serezha tries to find the objective truth, while his father keeps
rigidly to an utilitarian, Communist-Purpose oriented interpretation
of history. "... Ermak carried out the just conquest of Siberia. And
the rebellion of Shamil was also justly suppressed," Serezha repeats
his history teacher's words. "'Yes,' said Vladimir Petrovich
thoughtfully, 'we can't do without Siberia. And neither can we do

without the Caucasus. Oil. Manganese..." "When the English were conquering India, they also..." continues Serezha his train of thoughts. "'Stop these comparisons,' Vladimir Petrovich became agitated. 'The English are no rule for us. Where do we live? Is it in England?'"[73] And in an effort to instil in his son his own unquestioning faith Globov says: "...The main thing is our great Purpose. By it you must measure everything — from Shamil to Korea. Any means are sanctified by this Purpose, all sacrifices are justified by it. Millions, think, millions have perished for its sake, what only did the last war cost [us]! And you come here with all sorts of corrections — this is not just, that is not right!"[74]

The difference between Serezha and his father is further illustrated in the episode at the concert (chapter 1), where Tertz projects literary terms — "revolutionary Romanticism," "socialist Classicism" — which he had used in the essay onto his characters. To Serezha, a Romantic, music and reality grotesquely intertwined become visions of the Revolution which he admires and loves: "The music began to pour forth. It had multicolored patterns — like water in the street when gasoline is spilled. It was stormy, and was striving to get off the stage and into the concert hall. Serezha remembered that outside too rain was pouring, and quivered from pleasure. This was exactly how he imagined the revolution. The bourgeoisie were drowning in the most natural way. An elderly lady in an evening dress, struggling, climbed up a column. But the wave took her off. Her husband, a general, swam with a breast stroke, but sank also soon. The musicians themselves were already sitting in water up to their necks..."[75] His father, a "classicist," visualizes the same music as the orderly workings of Purpose: "...the music did not pour forth by itself, the conductor was guiding it. He erected dams, drew canals and aqueducts, and put the unbalanced elements into geometrically exact channels... The music was getting stormier and stormier. There were no longer waterfalls and rivers — they had long since frozen — icebergs came into motion as in the glacial age. One iceberg crashed against the other. Worlds and space were being displaced. A new age of granite and ice had come about."[76]

Serezha's dreams of heroic deeds, asceticism, and world revolution show him to be a potential "martyr of the revolution" — if there were a revolution. But his blueprint for a new society which he reveals to Katia at their meeting at the zoo (chapter 4) shows clearly that high goals will not be reached by high means as he claims, and that the idea of absolute freedom will result once again in absolute tyranny: ". . . The highest wages would be paid to cleaning women. Cabinet Ministers on the other hand would get a scanty share to insure absolute disinterestedness. The monetary system, torture, thievery — all would be abolished. Complete freedom would come about, and it would be so good that no one would put anyone into prison, and everybody would receive according to his needs. In the streets would be pasted Maiakovskii's posters. And also some others made up by Serezha: 'Beware! You may insult a man!' This was just in case they forgot themselves. But those who would forget, would be shot."[77]

To Katia's naive objections to zoos — she does not soar to such theoretical heights, and simply feels sorry for the caged animals — Serezha answers that "in the future society zoos would be completely rebuilt. Instead of these holes there would be large, airy cages. Barbed wire would be shaped like branches, so it would not be noticeable. The animals would feel nearly at liberty."[78]

Serezha remains the same romantic even after he is arrested and sentenced (Katia becomes scared of their "conspiracy" and confides it to the lawyer Karlinskii, and then to the school principal). And in Siberia, serving a sentence in a forced labor camp — ironically, together with the narrator, and with Rabinovich who had been overlooked by the amnesty following Stalin's death —

Serezha works diligently and still tries to put his ideals of a "new morality" into practice. "'My daily ration of 400 grams of bread,'" the narrator tells, "'was put together with the analogous ration of my friends. Rabinovich was in charge of all this bread, and when it was time for dinner, we divided 1 kilogram and 200 grams [of bread] into three parts. 'What use is this?' I asked with amazement. 'Still everyone eats his 400 grams and even less, because Rabinovich secretly bites off a piece from the portions of others.' 'Never mind, never mind,' Serezha encouraged me. 'The portion is not important, what is important is the principle of equal distribution of goods.'"[79]

But there are not only the "fathers and sons" in the story, but also a middle generation, which has neither the revolutionary ardor of the "sons," nor the faith of the "fathers," but is selfcentered, pragmatic and cynical. This middle generation, to whom Purpose lies only within themselves, is exemplified by the lawyer Iurii Mikhailovich Karlinskii, and by Globov's wife Marina.[80] In his epilogue the narrator with obvious irony classes "the lawyer Karlinskii, and the housewife Marina" among the positive characters, while the "child-murderer Rabinovich, the saboteur Serezha, and his accomplice Katia" are put into the category of negative characters. In actual fact, of course, there is no such division, just as the "hero," Globov, is not really the hero of the story. For the most interesting, original and psychologically complex character is Karlinskii — one of the first in Tertz's series of psychological "misfits," drunkards, thieves, graphomaniacs, madmen (cf. "The Fantastic Tales"). Outwardly, Karlinskii is more successful than any one of them, he is a talented lawyer, a clever manipulator of people who keeps his feet firmly on the ground, and never endangers his position. Although indirectly responsible for Serezha's ruin, he literally washes his hands "like Pontius Pilate" after receiving Katia's accusatory note, and forgets about both of them. Inwardly, however, Karlinskii seems to be patterned after the 19th century

Russian "superfluous" man who, as Tertz had said in the essay, stands *beyond* any Purpose. Karlinskii does not believe in traditional religion: ". . . When his father had died Iurii had wept hysterically, and everybody had thought that he was sorry for poor papa, but in reality he was sorry for himself, guessing his own mortality; and then, for a long time he kept asking everybody about life beyond the grave in the hope that it might exist. Why did they take away faith? Personal immortality has been replaced by Communism! But can there be any other purpose for a thinking man than he himself?"[81] He has no reverence for Marxism either. When during Marina's birthday party neo-Malthusianism and the problem of over-population are mentioned, Karlinskii comes to a piquant and even "orthodox" solution of the problem: to extract human embryos from their mothers' wombs and to condition them to fish that would be consumed by other humans: ". . . Next door to the abortarium there would be a fish cannery, cans in huge quantities. Some fish would be turned into sprats, others into sardines — according to national characteristics. And everything would be in keeping with Marxism. We will again return to the cannibalistic hors d'oeuvre. But not backwards, not to a primeval consumption of comrades equal to us, but so to speak, on a higher and more delicate basis. Developing along a spiral . . ."[82] Karlinskii's cynicism is matched by his ego-centrism, by his desire to be admired, known, to be in the center of the universe. During the celebration of the October Revolution he stays home on the pretext of illness and listens to foreign broadcasts: "Iurii was an aerial. But he wanted to be a transmitter, to send out mighty waves of whatever length. 'Attention! Attention! This is Karlinskii speaking. Listen only to me, me alone!'"[83] In order to escape from his feelings of emptiness and fear of death, Karlinskii finds a temporary diversion in the person of Marina whom he sets out to conquer. Since to Karlinskii as to Globov, "the goal justifies the means," he flatters, cajoles, and even humiliates himself before the hard and calculating Marina. "Let me be the unworthy means for your alljustifying beauty," he tells her during their meeting in a café. "Be my sun," he asks her, most appropriately, during a visit to the planetarium. "Your face is the center of the orbit around which I revolve." And while uttering these words he himself laughs at her, knowing full well that in reality he is the Purpose, and she only a means of relieving his insomnia. During his long drawn out combat with Marina, Karlinskii brings forth all his intellectual erudition, wit, and boldness, including some quasi-philosophical discussion of sex. "The sexual act . . . contains the primary ingredients of cognition," the brain being only "the cognitive appendix of our sexual organs," he tells her in a museum among still-lives and nudes. To this Marina professes complete indifference, knowing full well "that a beautiful woman must not be amazed even if Hegel himself were to demonstrate his theories to her."[84] Karlinskii's victory over Marina, however, is not so much due to his efforts as to her fear of being abandoned. It is significantly the day of Stalin's funeral, when Karlinskii reaches his goal and loses his illusions. For when Marina lies next to him, cold and ironic as ever, Karlinskii finds her repulsive and himself void of desire: "Iurii clenched his teeth and strained as if he were lifting weights of about three poods each. Finally, he evoked in his memory a pack of pornographic pictures which he had kept for a long time in a secret spot, and, going through the most indecent of them, prayed to God: 'O Lord, help me!'"[85] The essential hostility of the two sexes — a frequent motif in Tertz — seems also to reinforce Tertz's theoretical idea: the Purpose, finally reached, turns into its opposite and becomes meaningless.

Marina, finally, is a simplified version of the cynical ego-centrical Karlinskii, for she does not suffer his existential torments. Being the young wife of the elderly Prosecutor she accepts the material comforts which Globov offers her, while only barely tolerating him. She sees a Purpose only in herself, in the preservation of her beauty, and in a Narcissistic love of herself. The most important scene connected with her is the description of her 30th birthday (chapter 2) which she starts by exercising naked in front of a mirror. "In a severe, businesslike manner Marina checked her proportions. Do the buttocks sag, are there wrinkles on the neck? She unceremoniously kneaded her breasts, twisted her head, massaged her stomach. The mirror to her was a tool bench, a drawing board, a painter's easel — the working place of a woman who dreams of beauty. She was not trying to appear better looking, to show off. She labored decisively and with inspiration."[86] After having examined herself in all possible positions before the glass (while Globov stealthily looks on through the key hole) Marina reaffirms her belief: ". . . Nobody knows that a beautiful woman herself is worthy to be a Purpose. And all the rest: men, money, dresses, apartments, cars — are only the means, any means serving beauty."[87]

The historical ideology of the novel is concentrated in chapter 4, where the same Rabinovich whom Globov was prosecuting in reality appears to the latter in a grotesque dream as a guide through the Pushkin Museum of Fine Arts. Rabinovich first shows Globov a specimen of the human brain, contained in a jar of spirits, as the most lethal weapon of humanity: "I am afraid, citizen Prosecutor, that he may lose his mind from continuous thinking. The whole world civilisation would go to hell! We have split some ridiculous atoms, and are already worried. But here, in this jar, imagine the chain reaction of the brain. Explosions of ideas, hurricanes of dispersed thoughts. One just forgets to pay attention, and — what is the hydrogen bomb compared to it! Not only our humble planet, the whole galaxy would split into pieces. To say the truth, I am afraid for God . . ."[88] Then, Rabinovich demonstrates graphically

the various Purposes which had been mentioned in the essay —
Christianity, Individualism, Communism — in their invariable
deviations from the original ideals. Thus the Christian ideal of
love for one's neighbor resulted in destructiveness and intolerance: "... From the upper story hammering was heard. They were
chopping off the arms of some Venus of Milo. Then the smell of
overcooked meat was felt — heretics were being burnt. 'Now
they'll start slaughtering the Huguenots!' rejoiced Rabinovich."[89]
When Globov objects to such savagery among coreligionists, Rabinovich immediately transfers the problem to the contemporary
situation: "Is it possible to admit two Christianities? It's the same
nonsense as two socialisms. Take for example, our Tito ..." And
to this Globov dutifully gives the proper answer: "Tito is a fascist,
a spy, an American lackey!"[90] "Each decent Purpose consumes
itself. You strain your utmost to get to it, and barely you have
reached it — look — it is all reversed,"[91] explains Rabinovich the
processes of history. And when he begins to show Globov the result
of the most recent Purpose — Communism — the latter refuses to
look.

The tragic dichotomy between Purpose as an ideal and as
reality is brought out for the last time in the epilogue by the same
advocatus diaboli, Rabinovich. While digging ditches in Siberia,
he suddenly uncovers a sword with a handle in the shape of a
crucifix. "How do you like that?" Rabinovich asked his fellow-
prisoners. "Pay attention to where they applied God. To a murder
weapon — the handle! Don't you agree? He was a Purpose, but
became a means. In order to be more handy. And the sword — in
the other direction — was a means, but became a purpose. They
changed places. Oh, oh, oh! Where now is God, where is the sword?
In the eternal congelation are both the sword and God!"[92]

Although "The Trial Begins" is primarily a vehicle for Tertz's theoretical ideas, it also reflects some of his literary views, especially his plea for a new, non-socialist realist art, with fantasy, "conjectures and surmises." Especially striking in this respect is the prologue, which is a mixture of a Kafkaesque nightmare with a quasi-religious miracle: two silent, identical-looking plainclothesmen (Tolia and Vitia) suddenly appear in the narrator's room and search his belongings. One of them confiscates all his writings by passing "his palm over the first page, raking together letters and punctuation marks. A wave of the hand — and a violet heap was swarming in a lonely manner on the naked paper. One letter — it seems it was Z — moving its tail, quickly started to crawl away. But the dexterous young man caught it, tore off its legs, and squashed it with his nail."[93] At the moment when the narrator believes himself irrevocably lost and condemned, he is suddenly accorded grace in the form of a mysterious vision of the Master (Stalin): ". . . And above the houses, among the torn clouds, in the red rays of the rising sun, I saw a raised hand. In this fist which seemed frozen above the earth, in these thick, blood-filled fingers there was such great indestructible force that a sweet tremor of rapture seized me. Closing my eyes, I fell on my knees, and heard the voice of the Master. It came directly from heaven, and sounded at times like the furious bellowing of artillery weapons, at times like the tender murmuring of airplanes. The two plainclothesmen stood to attention. 'Rise, mortal. Don't turn your eyes from God's hand. No matter where you hide, no matter where you conceal yourself, it will overtake you everywhere, merciful and punishing. Look!'" The Master then points out to the narrator the hero whom he had chosen: "Did you recognize him, writer? It is he who is your hero, my beloved son and faithful servant, Vladimir [Globov] . . . Follow his every footstep, and do not leave him for a moment. In the moment of danger protect him with your body. And glorify!

Be my prophet! Let the light shine and let the enemies shudder at the word uttered by you!"[94] The epilogue, in which the narrator tells of his eventual exposure, has likewise a touch of a fantastic grotesque: "The story, which was finished except for the epilogue, became known in a certain high office. The cause of my downfall was, as could be expected, the dragnet mentioned earlier, which was installed in the sewage pipe of our house. The rough drafts which I conscientiously flushed down the toilet every morning, went immediately to the desk of Interrogator Skromnykh. And although the important personage whose order I had carried out (although perhaps not sufficiently correctly) had already died by this time, and was even subject to re-evaluation on the part of the general public, I was nevertheless prosecuted for slander, pornography, and the divulging of state secrets."[95]

Tertz's consciousness of form as part of his artistic credo is also felt in the artful composition of the story, some of its imagery and language. The chapters are often broken up, and the narrator jumps back and forth in space. Thus e.g. in chapter 1, the conversation between Marina and Karlinskii in the café is broken up by the conversation between Globov and Serezha, is resumed by Marina and Karlinskii, goes back to Globov and Serezha, and then again to Marina and Karlinskii. Similarly, in chapter 4, there is a threefold "jump": from the conversation of Serezha and Katia in the zoo, to Marina and Karlinskii in the museum, and to Globov (who first sees in a dream what happens in reality between Marina and Karlinskii, and later has his ideological dream involving Rabinovich). The connection between these sections is often made through phrases that are repeated by different characters. Thus Serezha in his conversation with his father (chapter 1) quotes Karlinskii as saying: "It all depends on your point of view," and Karlinskii's conversation with Marina in the next section starts with the same phrase: "It all depends on one's point of view, dear Marina

Pavlovna ..." Globov's lecture to his son which makes use of war experience is echoed by Karlinskii in the next section: "I give in, give in without battle, Marina Pavlovna." The imagery of fight and battle, in general, is quite prominent in the story, starting with the concrete combat of the sexes in which Marina and Karlinskii are engaged, going on to the description of a soccer match (chapter 3) which, in its turn, is compared to the drive for possessing a woman, and culminating in the image of an atomic explosion (chapter 2), when Marina tells Globov of her abortion: "The number of victims and the destruction are impossible to ascertain at the first moment. Everything has been wiped off the earth, and there is no one to fight with. But somewhere, on the outskirts, one man at least will survive ..."[96] There is, however, hardly any unity in the imagery, and Tertz tends to "borrow" as easily from life as from literature or the graphic arts. Thus e.g. there is a number of Biblical references as when Karlinskii imagines himself as the serpent handing Eve an apple (in reality he offers peaches to Marina, chapter 1), when he washes his hands like Pontius Pilate (chapter 6), trying to forget about Serezha and Katia for "Pontius Pilate probably thought little about Jesus Christ when he went to wash himself", when the narrator ponders about the magic of words (chapter 3) and their initial function: "In the beginning there was the word ..." The description of the fireworks on the occasion of the October Revolution is strongly suggestive of Maiakovskii's imagery: "The earth jumped up. Into the sky, bent backwards, rose steel pipes. This was the aorta which ruptured somewhere beyond the department store (Univermag). One needs a tourniquet. But they did not have time to put it on: other vessels broke. And multicolored blood splashed like a fountain toward the sky."[97] Tertz's interest in painting is reflected in the description of Marina's body as she is being undressed by Karlinskii: "... He could contemplate the complexity of her structure: arches, apses, cupolas. The onion domes of orthodox churches which were like breasts, and lancet gates like a belly pointing downward. But everywhere the guitar predominated: the shoulders, waist, pelvis. No wonder that Picasso liked the guitar and the violin as such — it was a woman's body in cross-section."[98]

Although Tertz refrains from linguistic experiments in the story, there is an occasional excursion into "non-realist," "transsense" language. Thus when Katia confides to Karlinskii their "conspiracy" he replies with a series of clichés, reduced ad absurdum: "One cannot permit that . . . All the world knows. Either or. Let's assume. Marxism, nihilism, spit-on-itism. France, action . . . -Mation, -cation, -zation, -nation, Nsip-ntsip ektiv. Humanization, Pferd!"[99]

An early work, "The Trial Begins" suffers perhaps from an excessive density of both ideological and formal material. In the "Fantastic Tales" ideology recedes into the background, while Tertz can give free reign to his rich imagination, and to create his peculiar phantasmagoric world.

3. "Fantastic Tales" ("Fantasticheskie povesti")

The "Fantastic Tales" are made up of four short stories, and a longer tale, "The Icicle", all of which were written between 1955 and 1961. To this can be added the short story "Pkhents", which appeared separately, but which by genre also belongs to the "Fantastic Tales."[100] The title of the collection clearly points to E.T.A. Hoffmann ("Fantasiestuecke in Callots Manier," 1814—15) whom Tertz had mentioned in his essay on socialist realism as one of his models for a new phantasmagoric art. Yet the connection with Hoffmann is general rather than specific, limited to a common predilection for combining strange happenings and weird characters

with a background of apparent reality. Tertz's interest in motifs of
the supernatural (ghosts and spirits, strange transformations,
obliteration of time and space) and various forms of psychic
"deviation" (madness, "doubles", morbid eroticism) connects him
with the Romantics in general, or with the Symbolists, for that
matter. There is an aura of "decadence" in the most general sense
of the word, of hopeless gloom, existential despair, which permeates
his stories. It is this strongly predominating "Romantic" layer
which probably prevented the prosecution from using the stories
against Tertz-Siniavskii at his trial. But in addition to this there is
also a "realistic" layer in the "Fantastic Tales" which connects the
stories with Soviet literature, as well as with 19th century Russian
literature. All of Tertz's tales are set in presentday Soviet Russia,
in a large city, presumably Moscow. There are references to specific
Soviet conditions, such as housing shortage, lack of food, lack of
privacy, censorship, the everpresent threat of repression etc. The
use of the "skaz" technique, the language of some of the characters
(a rather specific Soviet "jargon" that first appeared in print in the
early 1920's), political irony, rather obvious humor — all these
elements are strongly reminiscent of the early works of Mikhail
Zoshchenko, Il'f and Petrov, and Mikhail Bulgakov. But if Tertz's
manner is modern, his spiritual kinship is with the 19th century —
that "feminine and melancholy [century], filled with doubts,
internal contradictions, the gnawing of an unquiet conscience."[101]
There are clear echoes of Gogol', Dostoevskii, Chekhov in Tertz's
tales, while his basic themes — psychological and philosophical
problems — have a Dostoevskian tenor, and tend to delve into the
depths of the human spirit and into eternal existential problems.

a) "At the Circus" ("V tsirke"), 1955

"At the Circus" precedes, chronologically, Tertz's essay on
socialist realism as well as "The Trial Begins." This may account

for the relative simplicity of the story, and the lightness of its tone. For Tertz was as yet unencumbered by any stated intellectual "heresy" or clearly expressed literary theory. It is also, probably, one of the most "realistic" among the "Fantastic Tales." Nevertheless, the absence of a positive hero, or any moral lesson, the presence of some "risqué" erotic passages, and the use of some pronounced stylistic devices show Tertz's remoteness from socialist realism, and clearly point in the direction of his later stories. "At the Circus" revolves around Kostia, a young man of 25 years whose lack of education and professional skill prevent him from reaching the outstanding position in life which he desires. The symbol of success to him is the circus performer, who appears under brilliant lights and is greeted by an enthusiastic public. Although unable to approach him in skill, Kostia takes his inspiration from one of the circus performers, called the Manipulator ("an intelligent looking little gent with a foreign appearance") who is able to make things appear and disappear at will, and he becomes a thief. But Kostia's luck does not last, and when he takes part in the robbery of an appartment (which, by strange coincidence, is at that moment inhabited by the same Manipulator), he commits murder, and is brought to trial. While serving a sentence of 20 years of hard labor in Siberia, Kostia tries to escape and is shot while fleeing from prison camp.

Despite the simplicity of its plot, "At the Circus" is a rather interesting story in both ideas and form. It has a latent philosophical sub-stratum, a "double drawer", which becomes much stronger in Tertz's later stories. Kostia is, chronologically, the first in Tertz's gallery of "social misfits" — thieves, drunkards, and madmen — who are the heroes of the "Fantastic Tales." And there can be no doubt that he is a simplified version of Karlinskii in "The Trial Begins," and that he suffers (even though unconsciously) from a similar spiritual malaise as the latter: a desire to be

somebody, to startle the world by a marvellous trick, and a feeling
of emptiness due to lack of any belief. Getting drunk Kostia engages
time and again in long soulsearching conversations with an elderly
poor Jew, Solomon Moiseevich (again a simplified version of
Rabinovich in "The Trial Begins"), about the essence of things,
about the Russian character, about the soul. "Now then, Solomon
Moiseevich," Kostia would say, "since you are an educated man,
while I have not finished the 4th grade, answer me without delay:
what is the essence of everything? So that you would put this
essence in one word . . ." Or: ". . . Answer me, why am I a rogue
and thief, and why am I not at all ashamed of it? Now, tell me why
does a Russian always want to steal something? To steal or to drink?
Where does this quality of soul arise in a Russian?" And finally:
". . . What about my soul? Why was my soul given me??"[102] Unlike
Rabinovich, however, who has a whole (Tertz's) philosophical
theory at his disposal, Solomon Moiseevich cannot answer Kostia's
questions, and is only a silent listener who tries to placate or amuse
him with questions such as e.g. about the existence of God, thereby
hinting cleverly that "there were no gods or devils in this world,
although it would have been fun if they did exist."[103]

In the light of Tertz's collection of thoughts and aphorisms
("Thoughts at Random"), Kostia's drunkenness moreover is not
simply an expression of anti-social behavior, but assumes the aspect
of an unconscious, spiritual quest, not unlike that of some of
Dostoevskii's minor "sinners" (e.g. Marmeladov in *Crime and
Punishment*). By reaching the depths of degradation such characters,
according to Dostoevskii (and, apparently, also according to Tertz)
are simultaneously striving for the heights of human experience.
"Drunkenness is our basic national vice, and more — our *idée fixe*,"
Tertz says in his "Thoughts." "It is not from deprivation and
sorrow that the Russian drinks, but because of a certain need for
the *miraculous and extraordinary*, he drinks, if you wish, *mystically*,

trying to take the soul out of its earthly equilibrium, and to return it to its blessed, bodiless state. Vodka is the white magic of the Russian *muzhik;* — he prefers it decidedly to black magic — the feminine sex."[140] Kostia's erotic games with his girl-friend Tamara in the bathhouse, although satisfying at the moment, are still only temporary diversions, and cannot relieve him of his basic existential boredom and suffering.

Finally, again in the light of "Thoughts at Random," even Kostia's thievery becomes something like a Slavophile *apologia* of the Russian national character and a mark of strange spirituality: "... In connection with a tendency to steal (the absence of a firm faith in concrete connections among objects) (real'no-predmetnye sviazi) drunkenness gives us a vagabondish familiarity and puts us among other nations into the suspicious position of riffraff (liumpen) ... This gives us an undisputed advantage in comparison with the West, and at the same time puts upon the life and the strivings of the nation a stamp of instability, frivolous irresponsibility ..."[105]

If a basic tendency toward complex ideas is retained by Tertz later on, the formal devices in "At the Circus" — somewhat too contrived and obvious (again, repeated partly only in "The Trial Begins") — are not typical for Tertz's later stories. The most obvious formal device is the trick metaphor, which runs through the story as a kind of leitmotif. It originates from the description of a real "trick," the circus performance of the Manipulator, a rather funny passage with "nose" imagery suggestive of Gogol':[106] "With an innocent air he [the Manipulator] approaches a lady and pulls from under her hat a live white mouse. Then, a second, third, and thus — nine. The lady feels faint and says: 'Oh, I can't take this any longer!' and demands some water to calm herself. Then he runs up to her escort on the right side, and grabs him by the nose, carefully with two fingers like a barber. And with the free left hand

he takes out a wine glass from his pocket, and lifts it to the light so
that everyone can assure himself of its doubtless emptiness. Then
with a sharp motion he squeezes the nose of the gentleman and out
pours a golden drink, bubbling, with syrup, into the glass. And
without spilling anything, he politely offers it to the lady, who
drinks with pleasure and says 'merci' and everybody laughs and
claps his hands with pleasure."[107] After the performance Kostia
walks out "with that determined, springy gait which is common
only to conjurers and acrobats," and colliding in the crowd with
a man in a rich coat, he half-consciously carries out his first "trick":
"... and the coat opened up its furry interior even more, and the
wide, double-breasted jacket opened by itself, and all this happened
like a trick, without human interference."[108] Although this episode
marks the beginning of Kostia's new, better life which makes it
possible for him to enjoy the luxury of expensive restaurants, good
food and drink, he still dreams of a more ambitious, overwhelming
trick: "... And you must, you absolutely must show them something; some kind of *salto mortale*, or another amazing feat, or simply
find and utter a word — unique in this life — after which the
whole world will turn upside down, and in a moment will be
transformed into a supernatural state."[109] Instead of this marvellous
trick, however, Kostia shoots the Manipulator, half-accidentally,
out of fear of his miraculous powers, and this incident too is presented in terms of a trick metaphor: "He [the Manipulator] died
unobtrusively, without so much as a farewell wink, and left Kostia
bewildered by the trick which belonged in equal measure to them
both."[110] But it is only in the Siberian labor camp when Kostia has
finally the opportunity of performing his last, and most glorious
trick. And it is interesting to note that the actual setting of the camp
from which he tries to flee, with its barbed wire and light projectors
suggests to him the setting of the circus: "Kostia beheld an expanse
suffused with electric light, with kilometers of wire extended

beneath the vault of a world-wide circus. And the further he flew away from the initial point of his run, the more joyful and alarmed did his soul become. He was gripped by a feeling akin to inspiration, when every vein in your body leaps and cavorts, and cavorting awaits the onflow of this extraneous, magnanimous, supernatural power, which will throw you up into the air in one mighty leap, the highest and lightest in your light-weight life.

Ever closer, closer ... Now it will hurl you ... Now he will show them ...

Kostia leapt, turned over, and after having performed the long-awaited *salto,* fell with his face to the ground, shot through the head."[111]

In addition to the prominence of one specific device (the trick metaphor), the tenor of the tale is also somewhat unusual for Tertz and strongly suggestive of Zoshchenko. Presented in the "skaz" form,[112] the anonymous narrator[113] of "At the Circus" is rather close to the typical narrator of Zoshchenko's early stories: a half-educated man, a little brash but unsophisticated, whose language — a mixture of "high" and "low" language elements, current clichés and slang expressions — create rather humorous (and virtually untranslatable) effects. Tertz's narrator seems in his mentality to be close to Kostia, whose checkered career he follows with interest and even admiration. Thus, after the first theft, he begins to call his hero respectfully Konstantin Petrovich, and even to use plural verbs in connection with him: "... After which Konstantin Petrovich had the habit (imeli privychku — plural) of calming down, and having calmed down he would invite (priglashali — plural) to his table anyone who wished to come ..."[114] A rather typical example of the narrator's Zoshchenko-like style in its lack of logic and use of clichés (extremely difficult to render in English) is the description of Solomon Moiseevich: "Most often a certain sad man, elderly and modestly dressed, incidentally of Jewish nationality, although an alcoholic, would take a seat at his [Kostia's] table, who preserved on his emaciated chest a noble bow tie of blue color as token of [having received] higher eduction. His name was Solomon, and he would usually sit in a dark corner, under a palm tree, patiently waiting for a vacancy, for he did not dispose of any money, and they let him sit in the restaurant primarily because of his cultured appearance."[115] Another example of the narrator's style is Kostia's lamentation over his poor mama: "...he would weep and sob so that he would not be able to stop. And he would keep talking about his unhappy life, and he would remember his old mama, who — only three steps away — was lying on an iron bed and was dying from hunger, while he, the scoundrel, instead of running to her immediately bringing his mama some money for her cure, was hanging around here and drinking away all the money — up to the last kopeck — with the worst of scum..."[116] It might be added that Kostia's sick mama is only a figment of his lively imagination. The light, Zoshchenko-like tone with which the various episodes in Kostia's life are described make them appear funny; yet this tone seems to jar somehow with the essentially tragic content of the tale.

Even though "At the Circus" is not one of Tertz's best stories, its clear plot and swift pace make for interesting reading, while the description of Kostia's death in terms of a last "trick" is impressive in its starkness and finality.

b) "The Graphomaniacs" ("Grafomany"), 1960

Although chronologically "The Graphomaniacs" follow "The Tenants" and "You and I", it seems more appropriate to discuss this story at this point. For together with "At the Circus" it belongs to the two "realistic" stories among the "Fantastic Tales". There is even a superficial similarity in their respective plots: whereas the first story was concerned with an unsuccessful performer (Kostia), the second revolves around an unsuccessful writer (Straustin). However, the subject matter of "The Graphomaniacs" is infinitely more complex and involved than that of the first story, while its satirical tone sets it far apart from the less sophisticated narration of "At the Circus".

On the most general level, the theme of "The Graphomaniacs" is the problem of writing in general, the question of the borderline between talent or genius on the one hand, and sheer "graphomania" on the other. More specifically, the story is concerned with the plight of modern Russian writers, being encumbered with the unchallenged standards set by the "classical" writers of the 19th century; it is concerned with the question of "purposeless" creativity versus "directed" (socialist realist) art; and, last but not least, with the fate of the intellectual in the Soviet Union.

The narrator and simultaneously the hero of "The Grapho-maniacs" is an unsuccessful writer, Pavel Straustin. After having written novels and stories for some 20 years under conditions of extreme material deprivation, he still has not been able to publish a single work. Yet Straustin cannot give up, since he believes himself to be a great (if unappreciated) writer, and considers his similarly unlucky colleagues as mere graphomaniacs. This attitude comes out clearly during his accidental meeting with the poet Galkin whom he treats haughtily and whom he tries to impress by his imminent visit to a publisher. But at the government publishing office he is confronted with the usual humiliation: a pretty secretary informs him that his manuscript has been rejected and returned. A quarrel with his wife Zinaida who accuses Straustin of neglecting his family because of his graphomania, drives Straustin out of the house. Since he has no place to go to, he visits the poet Galkin and remains with him for a few days, watching various graphomaniacs come and go (for Galkin is somewhat of a maître among them). At

the end of that period Straustin deliberately picks a quarrel with
Galkin and leaves. After walking the streets all night, he returns to
his wife who vainly believes him "cured," and dreams of a new,
better life for all of them.

The question as to whether Straustin is a mere graphomaniac
or a talented writer remains unanswered and is, in a sense,
immaterial to the story. Chances are that his talent is slight. But he
knows and suffers all the torments connected with creativity. He
is keenly aware of the weight of tradition that stifles him, and
polemicizes against it. "It's the classical writers whom I hate most,"
he says to himself while returning home from Galkin's. "Already
before my birth they took up all vacancies, and I had to compete
with them, without being able to dispose even of a hundredth part
of their inflated authority. 'Read Chekhov, read Chekhov,' they
would repeat to me all my life, hinting tactlessly that Chekhov
wrote better than I . . ."[117] In another outburst, kept intentionally
on a low, naive and pragmatic level, the difference in the lifestyle
of the "classics" as opposed to the "moderns" points to the
impossibility of any literary competition (while at the same time
providing a clear commentary of the living conditions of Soviet
intellectuals): ". . . The classical writers of the 19th century had a
good life," Straustin ponders. "They lived on peaceful country
estates, had a steady income, and sitting on glassed-in verandas, in
intervals between balls and duels, would write their novels, which
were published immediately in every corner of the globe. They
knew some foreign language from birth, were taught various
literary styles and devices in lycées, travelled abroad where they
refreshed their brains with new material, and, as for their children,
they were handed over to a governess, while their wives were sent
off to dances or to the dressmaker, or shut away in the country.

But nowadays, just try to be inspired, when your organism
asks for food, and your head is burdened by the thought of how to

get to the necessary goal, how to overcome the hurdle put up on your path by rascal-graphomaniacs who entered literature by devious ways and closed up behind them all entrances and exits. Where to get your three meals a day? And then — you have to pay for gas and electricity, and your shoesoles are worn, and you have to settle up with the typist for 200 pages of typescript at a ruble per page . . . O the misery of such existence!"[118]

Straustin tries to be a realist, even a socialist realist. This is evidenced by his themes (the Revolution and Civil War, both of which are personally unknown to him), by his optimistic titles ("In Search of Happiness," "The Sun Rises over the Steppe," "Man"), by his dislike of "modern" poetry (such as Galkin's), and his attentiveness to realistic details (e.g. when he scrutinizes Galkin at the beginning of the story). When a thought occurs to him, he immediately tries to utilize it for literary purposes: "The breath of an approaching storm was felt in the air. I like this. I must remember and utilize it: 'The breath of an approaching storm was felt in the air.' With this sentence I will conclude my novel *In Search of Happiness*."[119] Yet despite his attempts to follow the official demands, he does not succeed — perhaps because an art form artificially forced upon a writer becomes nothing but a dead weight around his neck, and can never come to life.

Despite Straustin's very real frustrations as an artist, despite the misery of his living conditions (a squalid one room dwelling with kitchen smells and continuous noises from a trumpet player practicing upstairs) Tertz's representation of him is strongly satirical at times. He is shown as malicious, egocentrical and envious to the point of paranoia. While waiting in the publisher's office, he spitefully eyes the pretty secretary who ignores him, and dreams how he would seduce her in a luxurious hotel suite if he were famous: ". . . Not because it would be very necessary, but simply for the sake of justice."[120] His wife's unhappiness does not touch him, and while she laments their life, he coldly regards her, and thinks how it was possible that "this strange, middle-aged, unattractive woman, exhausted by women's diseases, poorly dressed, and always rushing somewhere"[121] was his wife. He even wishes that she would find somebody else to marry, or that she would die, for then "it would be quiet and spacious in the room, and one could peacefully write in the evenings."[122]

Straustin's envy extends, beyond the "classical" writers, to most of his contemporaries, and even to his 6 year old son. When he starts reading some contemporary Soviet writers during his stay at Galkin's, he suddenly discovers traces of what he considers to be his own thoughts in their works: ". . . For instance, [Konstantin] Fedin wrote: 'The road led to a wide garden and vegetable plantation.' But in my story of 1935, entitled 'The Sun rises over the Steppe' there was — I remember it exactly — such a phrase: 'The road led to a wide field planted with appletrees.' Only in my case the apple trees, I remember, were blooming and glittering in the sun with their pink blossoms. But Fedin, in order to cover up his plagiarism, abolished all the beauty of my blooming trees, and thus immeasurably spoiled the scene. But still, my bit, even in this distorted way, helped him to make a brilliant career quickly, and now without shame he used the fruits of glory which in actual fact belonged to me alone."[123] Straustin then checks upon other authors, and no matter who it is, whether Leonov, Paustovskii, Fadeev, or Sholokhov, he finds everywhere traces of himself, "submerged in a mass of silly, nonsensical texts."[124] Even in François Mauriac, Straustin finds four details taken from one of his early stories, entitled "Man," and after racking his brain for some time, he comes to the conclusion that "the robbers" had sent copies of his works abroad! Straustin's quarrel with Galkin is based on his suspicion that the latter has been stealing phrases from his unpublished manuscript while he slept.

When Straustin's 6 year old son (whose first name, incidentally, is also Pavel) shows him a fairy tale which he had just composed, Straustin is at first pleased by the fact that the child has inherited his literary talent. But then he grows alarmed, remembering that "geniuses have no posterity. The children of Leo Tolstoi had no right to write. The Dumas' do not count: both are no good, especially Dumas fils . . ."[125] And fearful, lest in 200—300 years' time people may confuse his writings with those of his son, he strictly forbids him to write, consoling him with the promise that he may eventually copy his papa's manuscripts.

Straustin's literary image as an unsuccessful "socialist realist" is counterbalanced by the image of the poet Galkin, a "modernist" (and thus an opponent of socialist realism), and a believer in "purposeless" art. His poetic vocabulary ("hairy legs," "pilasters," "Chrisanthemums"), the title of his unpublished collection of poetry ("In the Whale's Womb" — 19th book of verse), his preoccupation with making books of the most unusual shapes, as e.g. that of a sea-urchin, seem to stamp him an epigone of the various artistic "-isms" (such as Futurism, Cubism, etc.) which were flourishing in Russia in the early 20th century. When Straustin comes to him, he finds him making a book "that opened up like an accordion, and was covered inside with poems of an abstract character. Other books — in the shape of a cube, a pyramid, and an egg — had been produced a month earlier with the cooperation of the same Galkin who saw in these productions the synthesis of poetry, painting, and sculpture."[126] It is interestingly the absurd Galkin who is the "theoretician" of literature in the story. Literature as seen by Galkin, is the result of graphomania, "an incurable evil urge to produce verse, plays, novels — in defiance of the whole world . . ." "They say," Galkin tells Straustin, "'to imprint oneself,' 'to express one's personality,' but in my opinion, every writer is occupied with only one thing: self-elimination. This is the reason why we toil in

the sweat of our brow, use up wagon loads of paper — with the
hope of eliminating ourselves . . ."[127] The question of greatness and
fame is secondary to this involuntary, irrational, purposeless urge,
in Galkin's opinion, and is often decided by chance, luck. He even
pays an ironic tribute to Soviet censorship which fosters graphomania: ". . . Abroad it is simpler, merciless. A lord will publish a book
of *verse libre*, and one can see immediately — it's trash. Nobody
reads it, nobody buys it, and the lord turns to some useful occupation — energetics, stomatology . . . But we live all our lives in
pleasant ignorance, are full of hope. And this is wonderful! The
state itself, deuce take it, gives you the right — the priceless right! —
to consider yourself an unacknowledged genius . . ."[128] It is Galkin
who makes a speech to his fellow-graphomaniacs assembled in his
room, and encourages them to keep on writing: ". . . He [Galkin]
termed graphomania the foundation of foundations and the beginning of beginnings, and called it the swampy soil from which the
purest sources of poetry issue. This soil, said Galkin, is overflowing
with moisture. It has no way out, said Galkin. The time would come,
said Galkin, when it would burst out of the depths and would
flood the world,"[129] Straustin records his speech. And in a funny
paraphrase of a Communist slogan, Galkin promises his followers
that "he who had been a nobody . . . would become somebody, and
let there be insufficient paper for all, we will cover the walls of the
houses, and the bare pavements of the streets with texts in verse and
prose . . ."[130] Although the efforts of Galkin are even more hopeless
than are Straustin's, it becomes clear that by following his
inclinations in a free, modern art he remains true to himself, and is
ultimately the happier of the two writers. And despite the fact that
Straustin and Galkin are ideologically miles apart, they come
together, in the final analysis, as captives of the same creative urge,
the same malaise — be it graphomania, or literary genius. There
seems to be even a touch of sympathy on Tertz's part for them,

ridiculous and personally unattractive as they may be. The story
ends on a conciliatory note, while Straustin's last words have a ring
of pathos and sincerity which seem to echo Tertz's own feelings. Not
only is Straustin unable to stop writing (despite promises to his
wife), he now encourages his son to follow his literary inclinations:

"Write, Pavel, write," he says. "Don't be afraid. Let them
laugh at you and call you a graphomaniac. They are graphomaniacs themselves. All around us are graphomaniacs. There are many,
many of us, more than are necessary. And we live in vain and we
die in vain. But someone of us will make it. Either you, or I, or
somebody else. He will make it, he will carry [his idea] through.
Write, Pavel, compose your fairy tales about your funny dwarfs.
And I will write about mine . . . You and I will make up so many
fairy tales. You cant't count them all. Only look — don't tell it to
mama . . ."[131]

Narrated in the first person form by Straustin, "The Graphomaniacs" is, as already mentioned, quite realistic both in subject
matter and in form. There seem to be some intentional echoes of
Chekhov,[132] (who also has some ideological importance in the
story), as e.g. in the subtitle "Tales about my life" ("Iz rasskazov
o moei zhizni"), in the presentation of the tale as a kind of
Chekhovian "slice of life" — without beginning or an end, even
perhaps in a certain atmosphere of hopelessness and gloom that is
often associated with Chekhov's stories. There are, however, also
a few fantastic "twists" which Tertz uses in some of his other tales
as well. For example, Straustin overhears the recitations of various
other "graphomaniacs" in Galkin's room as a simultaneous,
nonsensical stream of disjointed sentence: "Above us the sky with
the smile of a woman and violet like a prune of a lieutenant by the
name of Greben' [Comb] was resting on the green grass. General
Ptitsyn [Bird], not wiping off scant soldierly tears which were
streaming down his cheeks, commanded: 'I love you, dear Tania,'

and their lips met in a fiery kiss. And he felt in his soul such a cheese cake (vatrushka s tvorogom) and pie with mushrooms (pirogi s gribami) and a half dozen hard, cold as ice, cucumbers which smelled of fresh dill and were made early in spring, when one feels like weeping from joy together with nature and shouting: 'O Russia, where are you rushing to?' blessing the first fluffy, tender, rosy snow onto the black, dirty, slippery road . . ."[133] Straustin's graphomanic urge acquires also some strange, supernatural overtones, suggestive of powers beyond his control, as seen during his walk home: "Suddenly it seemed to me that I was not walking along the street by myself, but that somebody's fingers were guiding me, as a pencil is guided along the paper. I was walking in a small uneven handwriting, I was following, as fast as I could, the movement of the hand which was composing and writing down on the pavement and on these deserted streets, and these houses with some of its windows still lighted, and on myself, all my long long unsuccessful life . . ." And in an impotent gesture of defiance Straustin turns to the sky and says: "Hey you there, graphomaniac! Stop writing! All that you have written is no good. How vapid is all that you have composed. It's impossible to read you . . ."[134]

A strange tale, without clear structural connections, "The Graphomaniacs" may best be regarded as a series of diverse literary utterances. For the theme of literature and of the writer occupies an important place in Tertz's works, starting with "The Trial Begins," and ending with "The Icicle" and *Liubimov*.

c) "The Tenants" ("Kvartiranty"), 1959

With "The Tenants" the "fantastic" Tertz comes to the foreground. Although the setting of the tale is real enough — a Soviet communal apartment, filled with intrigue, mutual suspicion and distrust typical for this sort of enforced collective living[135] — it is presented in an "estranged" manner, through the eyes of a house spirit (domovoi). The question as to whether the narrative of Nikodim Petrovich (the house spirit masquerading under the guise of an elderly house-manager) should be accepted at its face value, as an excursion into a world of pure fantasy (with strong overtones of Russian folklore); whether it is a satirical, and at times symbolical inversion of reality, or whether it may be perhaps a psychological study of a hallucinating alcoholic (the silent listener who, incidentally, is a writer), is left open as so often in Tertz. The second interpretation, however, seems to be more in tune with Tertz's artistic vision and predilection.

"The Tenants" is a story with two lines of development, a tale within a tale. One is concerned with the relations of Nikodim Petrovich, the house spirit, with a new tenant, Sergei Sergeevich (the alcoholic writer) whom he visits four times during the course of the story, trying to persuade him to leave the apartment, since all its other inhabitants are witches and evil spirits bent on his destruction. However, despite all efforts on Nikodim Petrovich's part, he is unable to move Sergei Sergeevich (who does not utter a single word throughout the story), and at the end the two protagonists remain both physically and psychologically exactly where they were at the beginning.

The second story, interwoven into this rather static structure, is both dramatic and even more fantastic. It is told to Sergei Sergeevich by Nikodim Petrovich in installments (to heighten the reader's suspense), and illustrates the dangers which might befall him should he choose to stay on at the apartment. It concerns Ninochka and Nikolai, a completely normal young couple, who had lived in the apartment prior to Sergei Sergeevich, and who were destroyed by the rest of its inhabitants. Not only did the other "witches" persecute Ninochka in the communal kitchen, she eventually had an affair with another man, Anchutker[136] (a forest spirit in Nikodim Petrovich's opinion) who got her pregnant, and then turned her into a rat in order to get rid of her. She still runs around the apartment in that shape, while poor Nikolai ended up in an insance asylum.

The most distinctive feature of "The Tenants" is, as already mentioned, a kind of inversion of reality, whereby seemingly normal events are presented in terms of fantasy and vice versa. An example of the first type are e.g. such scenes as Ninochka's experiences in the communal kitchen — an ironic commentary on Soviet living conditions, presented in an "estranged" manner: "Can you imagine the picture? The kitchen. Smoke and commotion. In the smoke these witches are swaying, grabbing each other by their disshevelled locks. They spit in each other's faces at close distance. They utter bad words very distinctly: 'Witch! Strumpet!' 'You yourself are a witch! Where did you ride off last night on a lavatory pan?'"[137] The beginning of the affair between Ninochka and Anchutker which seems perfectly natural, is also seen by Nikodim Petrovich in terms of magic and witchcraft: ". . . Kolia stood it for a long time, but one day he said [to Ninochka]: 'Go to the devil [leshii, wood spirit], Ninochka. I am tired of these scandals.' And as soon as he pronounced these fateful words, Anchutker walks into their room. As if on business, to borrow a cigarette. And he looks intently at Ninochka, and Ninochka looks at Anchutker, and they liked each other very much at that moment . . . In one word, she was exactly to his taste, and there started between them meetings, pinchings, tender scratchings and all that sort of thing. She became a real witch . . ."[138]

Fantastic statements or events, on the other hand, are presented in a completely matter-of-fact manner, as perfectly "normal." Such is e.g., Nikodim Petrovich's lengthy pseudoscientific discourse on the presence of waternymphs in the city, who have been forced to leave their natural habitat because of the advance of technology:

"... Brooks, rivers, lakes began to reek of chemical substances. Methylhydrate, toluene. Fishes simply died and floated belly upward. But these [the waternymphs] would emerge, catch a breath somehow, and there would be tears — you would not believe it! — of grief and disappointment in their eyes. Saw it myself. All over their luxurious bosom there would be ringworm, exzema and even, if you'll pardon my immodesty, sings of recurrent venereal disease. Where can one hide? — They did not think long, but followed the wood spirits and witches — to the city, to the capital ... You yourself must have heard. You turn on the kitchen tap, and out of it come sobs, various splashings, curses. You think — whose antics are these? It's their voices, the waternymphs. One will get stuck in the washbasin, and will start being naughty, and will start sneezing! ..."[139]

Nikodim Petrovich's strange appearance in the writer's room at the beginning of the third conversation (he crawls in through a crack) and his subsequent camouflage as a wine glass, are also presented as quite real: "What suitable objects have you got here? Aha! Let me be a glass. And you sit down at the table as if you were drinking. If anyone looks in — talk to yourself. Let them think that you are drunk. It is safer that way. Now come here: I am already on the table. You see, you had three glasses, and now you have four. But no, not that one! How unobservant you are, really! Here I am, here! Next to the plate. Oh! Don't touch me with your hands! Yor may drop me on the floor and break me. My bones ache as it is ..."[140]

The image of the central figure of the tale, Nikodim Petrovich (if indeed he does exist, and is not a product of Sergei Sergeevich's alcoholic imagination), shows the same illogical and unexpected intertwining of reality and fantasy. At first, his "humanness" is stressed, even though he does have occasional quirks: e.g., at the end of the first conversation he offers to perform a "trick" by disappearing in thin air. He presents himself to Sergei Sergeevich as an elderly housemanager in student dormitories and communal apartments, semi-educated, although with a smattering of "culture": in the course of the conversation he mentions such writers as Fenimore Cooper, Eugène Sue, Mayne Reid, Heinrich Heine, and last but not least, Leo Tolstoi. The love-triangle — Nikolai, Ninochka, Anchutker — is compared by him to the plot of *Anna Karenina!* In the course of the narrative, presented in the *skaz* form, Nikodim Petrovich is revealed as kind, humorous, and wise with age and experience. His colloquial language and humor considerably enhance the illusion of his human stature, while at the same time they lighten a sad tale. His description of the other inhabitants of the communal apartment is a masterpiece of humor and mystification. Thus a young woman by the name of Sofia Frantsevna Vinter who "runs around in a cotton morning gown, does aquatic exercises from morning to evening" (in the communal bathroom) and sings the "Lorelei" in German is, in Nikodim Petrovich's opinion, a waternymph. "For heaven's sake don't run after her," he warns Sergei Sergeevich. "She'll tickle you to death. And as to something more substantial, I'll tell you that she has fish blood, and everything else obout her is fish-like. Only the appearance is that of a lady — just to tempt you."[141] The proofs against Anchutker's "humanness" are equally comical: ". . . Have you ever seen such wool [hair] on a man?" Nikodim Petrovich exclaims. "And his complexion? Where will you find a man with a skin that is blue to such a degree? And he has a somber expression, and his boots are size 47, and are always mixed up: the right boot is on the left foot, and the left on the right."[142] A further sign that Anchutker is a forest spirit in Nikodim Petrovich's opinion is the fact that he keeps reading novels about the forest (Korolenko's *The Forest Roars*, Leonov's *The Russian Forest)*, and that he works in a forestry department!

The clue to Nikodim Petrovich's real identity as a house spirit, and the reason for his sympathy for Sergei Sergeevich (and Ninochka and Nikolai before him) comes out in the second conversation, in which he explains the difference between him and "them": ". . . It's the ignoramuses, illiterate, uncultured peasant women who say that a house spirit is, as they say, much the same as a forest spirit. You are wrong! It's a completely different profession. It's impossible not to see the basic differences in this question. The house spirit is used to the house, to the smell of man, to warmth. From the beginning of time. He has nothing to do with devils and witches. Perhaps, you think they share a common nature. Don't say so! Never mind nature! Man, for example, has also evolved from the ape. However, subsequently he developed into an independent species. He deals with apes only in Africa, and in the zoo . . ."[143]

And as the story progresses, this distinction between Nikodim Petrovich and Sergei Sergeevich on one hand, and "them" on the other seems to acquire a different, symbolic meaning, and to become tied up with the motif of danger and persecution. Nikodim Petrovich's language shifts to a different, judicial terminology, transforming the fantastic aura of the tale back into a realistic, namely that of a totalitarian state. Rushing to the writer in great agitation, Nikodim Petrovich claims that the other "witches" have discovered their friendship and that "an investigation is on the way." "I know they want to put me on trial. For betraying their secrets," Nikodim Petrovich says. And quoting a higher official among the witches, he continues: ". . . We [the witches] . . . trusted him, but he has periodic contacts with foreign elements. We . . . forgave him the incident with the newlyweds, but now he again starts a friendship with someone he is not supposed to. And his new friend is a writer who puts down on paper everything he says. There can be unpleasant consequences. The chatterbox must be

punished so as to make an example. And the writer we'll take on
separately. Since he is an alcoholic he will soon start seeing real
devils . . ."[144]

In a terrified vision Nikodim Petrovich sees himself being
separated from his writer-friend, and sent under the floor, "to
join the microorganisms," or being launched into the sewage system,
where he will be forced to circulate until the end of time. As to
the writer, his fate in Nikodim Petrovich's opinion, is equally
terrible, for he will be driven into insanity. And while Nikodim
Petrovich frantically attempts to induce the drunken writer to
get up and to save himself either through flight, or prayer (!),
"they" are heard coming ever closer: ". . . They are coming for
me. And for you too, Sergei Sergeevich. For you too. For you
too."[145]

This strange "twist" at the end of the story whereby fantasy
turns into symbolic "reality" is not unusual for Tertz, who delights
in mixing up various levels of existence and imagination. And it
seems futile to try to pinpoint exactly what Tertz is trying to say
in this tale, and whether Nikodim Petrovich is a fantastic "reality,"
or a kind of romantic "double" of the drunkard Sergei Sergeevich.
Tertz's complexity and intentional ambiguity permit a variety of
interpretations. What seems important in analyzing works such as
this one is the skill with which he manipulates his material, and the
persistence of certain motifs — the image of the writer, literature,
danger, persecution — which seem to point to the autobiographical
core of Tertz's art.

d) "You and I" ("Ty i ia"), 1959

In "You and I" Tertz goes to the limits of his complex fantasy,
both in terms of the ultimate meaning of the story, and its formal
(and clearly intentional) "difficultness." The result is not altogether

felicitous. For although most of Tertz's fantastic tales are complex, they usually do have a "key" which puts them within the framework of Tertz's very personal, paradoxical weltanschauung (which is nevertheless consistent in its own terms). "You and I" seems to lack this consistency, and seems to be more of a grotesque and macabre exercise on a theme by Gogol' or Dostoevskii. One can suggest various possibilities for interpreting the tale; if it has a "key," however, it is known only to the author himself.

The basic plot of "You and I" is quite simple and yet dramatic. Its hero, Nikolai Vasil'evich, a clerk in an unnamed ministry, is invited to a silver wedding anniversary celebration by his elder colleague, Genrikh Ivanovich Graube. Nikolai Vasil'evich suspects that the celebration is only a pretext for politically compromising him, and therefore he is on guard throughout the evening, pours his vodka under the table instead of drinking, and weighs each of his words. The party ends with a minor scandal, and Nikolai Vasil'evich leaves with the girl Lida whom he pretends to have fallen violently in love with. Soon after the party Nikolai Vasil'evich takes leave of absence from his work (under the pretext of a trip to Yalta to cure his ulcers). In reality, however, he locks himself in his room, and succumbs even further to his fears and suspicions. A chance encounter with Graube (Nikolai Vasil'evich sneaks out of the house to buy some food), and the reappearance of Lida (who wants to see him again) at his apartment door drive Nikolai Vasil'evich into a state of frenzy, and he ends up by slitting his throat with a razor blade.

The connection of the story with those of Gogol' (or the early Dostoevskii) is one of atmosphere, allusions, subtle parallels. Except for a few chance remarks (e.g. on the scarcity of poultry in meat-stores), and an aura of political conspiracy and danger suggestive of Soviet reality, the story could be timeless. The setting of tension and suspense, the minor "scandal" at the end of the

party, the final tragic dénouement, the choice of names — an
obvious allusion to Gogol' in the case of the hero, "funny" Russian
or German names (Lobzikov, Genrikh Ivanovich Graube) — all
these are devices to be found in those two writers. The figure of
Nikolai Vasil'evich himself — that of a timid, middle-aged,
inconspicuous clerk — seems to be modeled on Gogol"s and
Dostoevskii's sometimes "humble and meek" and sometimes mad
clerks. And like Gogol"s Poprishchin ("Notes of a Madman") and
Dostoevskii's Goliadkin ("The Double"), Tertz's Nikolai
Vasil'evich appears normal only on the surface. There is little
information given about him, except for the facts that he is ginger-
haired, slightly freckled, neat in appearance, and that — being a
bachelor — he occasionally visits "certain" houses, "paying
modestly, according to the rate, 25 and 30, sometimes even 50
rubles in cash, and receiving without sin, by mutual agreement, the
reward due . . ."[146] But as the story unfolds, it becomes increasingly
clear that he is mad, suffering from a severe case of persecution
mania which leads to his destruction. One part of the story, which
revolves around him, is a "carefully executed examination of
paranoia."[147]

The lighter, grotesque (and comprehensible) aspect of the tale
is connected with the person of Nikolai Vasil'evich and his reactions
to the world around him. Having come, much against his will, to
the anniversary party, Nikolai Vasil'evich sees every move, every
word of the host and the other guests as signs of conspiracy against
him: the guests click their knives and forks in a secret code,
Lobzikov (one of the guests) bites off the side of a duck, indicating,
metaphorically speaking, that a similar fate was in store for the
hero, Graube's ears stick out "like headphones" on both sides, while
his eyes "rove microscopically" over Nikolai Vasil'evich's face.

Even more, believing the whole affair to be only a trap for
him, Nikolai Vasil'evich does not believe in the identity of Mme.

Graube herself, but thinks her to be a man in disguise "carefully washed, made up with powder and lipstick — and produced as a lady with a 25 year record [of marital service]."[148] This, in Nikolai Vasil'evich's opinion, is the reason why Genrikh Ivanovich had a look of disgust when he "kissed her — or, rather, him — in public, on the proffered, muscular lips."[149] The respective wives of Lobzikov and Polianskii (other guests) are, in Nikolai Vasil'evich's view, also "fakes," and he calculates not without some feeling of pride that the whole affair (including food, drink, and "false" clothing) must have cost a pretty penny to those who are out to ensnare him. Since the only female person of whose identity Nikolai Vasil'evich is sure is Lida, the librarian in the ministry, a skinny, unattractive but accessible girl (Graube, Lobzikov, and Polianskii all had affairs with her), he starts a violent flirtation with her, pretending to be drunk. When the "spy", Vera Ivanovna, voices her amazement at his behavior, Nikolai Vasil'evich assures her that he is quite a lady-killer, and to prove his words (and simultaneously to convince himself of the fact that Vera Ivanovna is a "fake"), he pokes at her breasts, finding (just as he thought) nothing but "an inflated rubber cushion." While Vera Ivanovna squeals from fright, and Genrikh Ivanovich turns green ("over the failure of his provocation," as Nikolai Vasil'evich believes), he escapes from the party with Lida. "I can see right through you, Genrikh Ivanovich," he ominously shouts at his flabbergasted host, and slams the door in his face.

It is obvious that Nikolai Vasil'evich's mania is misplaced as regards the Graubes and their guests. Yet he is right in feeling watched. For he is watched by a mysterious narrator, the "I" of the story who contributes so much to the complexity of the tale both in content and form. Here, the earlier echoes of Gogol' and Dostoevskii become transformed and distorted into a macabre, mad fantasy. The mysterious "I" is first introduced in a street setting (chapter 2) where he watches the snow and various passersby: a

twelve year old boy with skates, a gentleman by the name of
Nikolai Vasil'evich (but a different one from the hero of the story)
hurrying to a rendezvous with a brunette.[150] Gradually, it becomes
evident that his vision is limitless, both in time and space, and that
he is watching all people "steadily . . . penetratingly and vigilantly."
Yet as long a people are unaware of his presence nothing happens.
Not so Nikolai Vasil'evich, the hero, who even in the empty, snow-
swept street (on his way to the Graube party) "attracted attention
by constantly looking over his shoulder. Even indoors, surrounded
by food and drink, receiving the hospitality of a kind host, he
behaved like a criminal who might be caught and unmasked at any
moment."[151] Nikolai Vasil'evich himself, while sitting at the Graube
dinner table, has the feeling that "in addition to everything else . . .
somebody invisible and all-seeing had looked at that moment
(through the window, from the wall, or through the wall?)"[152] at
him and at all those present. From that evening on Nikolai
Vasil'evich and the narrator become like "prisoners, unable to take
their glazed eyes off each other." Strangely enough, the narrator
does not wish any harm to Nikolai Vasil'evich and is apparently,
as unhappy in this fatal psychic connection as the latter. And while
Nikolai Vasil'evich, shut up in his room, sees only detached eyes
"brown, grey, blue — flying around the room winking their
eyelashes" at him and preventing him from sleep, the narrator
decides to intervene. Assuming the guise of another man (Ippolit),
he appears at the place of action where Lida is besieging Nikolai
Vasil'evich's room. (The latter won't let her in, since by now he is
convinced that she too is in "their" service.) Inviting Lida to a
restaurant, "Ippolit" tries to divert himself and her from the
unfortunate Nikolai Vasil'evich. But Lida's thoughts are with the
latter, she constantly compares "Ippolit" to him, and finally utters
the fateful phrase: ". . . Please shave off your beard. Please, dear,
for me. Take a razor and shave it off!"[153] And though "Ippolit"

reverts now to the extreme measure of making love to Lida on top of a deserted staircase landing in order to disengage their mental connection with Nikolai Vasil'evich, it does not help: "It was too late. I entered into your brain, into your fevered consciousness, and all your last secrets which I did not even want to know, were revealed to me. You jumped up from the chair. All witnesses of your crime were gathered. Aha! Got them! You brandished the ready razor blade at me, at Lida, at the whole world . . ."[154] And as Nikolai Vasil'evich cuts his throat, the narrator regains a calm which he had not known for some time. "Everything became dark and quiet. I stopped seeing you. You no longer existed."[155]

The meaning of the mysterious, omniscient, allseeing (but apparently not almighty!) "I" is extremely difficult to decipher. It has been interpreted as one half of a "double personality who speaks now in one voice, now in another," while the internal conflict between "you" and "I" is supposed to have overtones of a homo- and heterosexual struggle.[156] Another critic who considered the story from a literary-religious (rather than psychopathological) point of view suggested that the "I" represents "omniscient God,"[157] to which the epigraph from Genesis XXXII, 24 ("And Jacob was left alone and there wrestled a man with him until the breaking of the day") seems to give additional weight. However, both these interpretations seem to miss the point somewhere. Although there are doubtlessly elements of a Romantic (Gogolian, Dostoevskian) "double" in the "I", this "I" seems to be more than just another aspect of Nikolai Vasil'evich. The epigraph, as already mentioned, points to a superior being. At one point the narrator says to Nikolai Vasil'evich: ". . . You are only you because it is I who addresses you. Only having been seen by God you have become man."[158] But is this "I" God in the literal sense? Tertz's vision, at least as far as it is possible to judge from his fiction up to that point, is hardly religious in a conventional, orthodox sense.

It appears rather that what Tertz wanted to express was a philosophical idea (distorted by his favorite phantasmagoric devices),
namely, the relativity of existence (Nikolai Vasil'evich), which is
conditioned by the presence of consciousness ("I"). Most people
live without being conscious of this dichotomy. But Nikolai
Vasil'evich's self-consciousness reaches such gigantic proportions
("mania grandiosa" the narrator terms it) that he cannot go on
living. Yet when he dies, the consciousness (a kind of soul?)
continues to exist beyond the body and finds peace. As already
mentioned, however, the story is too complex to have one definite
interpretation, and what Tertz ultimately wanted to say will
remain a mystery.

The extreme complexity of the content of "You and I" is
matched by its formal devices. There are constant shifts in narrative
voice, combined with a kind of "surrealist" technique in which
many different events are presented as taking place simultaneously,
or are "fragmented" into disjointed images. To give only a few
examples of this: chapters 1,3 are told in the second person form
(referring to Nikolai Vasil'evich), chapters 2 and 4 in the first
person form (referring to the "I"), while chapters 5 and 6 are
mixed — there is a first person and also third person narrative
(the narrator now referring to Nikolai Vasil'evich as "he" rather
than "you"). This fragmentation is probably consistent with the
role of the narrator's wide, panoramic vision: "It was snowing. A
fat woman was cleaning her teeth. Another woman, also fat, was
cleaning fish. A third was eating meat. Two engineers were playing
a Chopin duet on the piano. In the maternity wards four hundred
women were simultaneously giving birth. An old woman was
dying. . ."[159] Not only does the narrator see all these events
simultaneously, he at times fractures his vision, putting disparate
pieces together in a bizarre, surrealistic manner: ". . . [He] ran with
a suitcase in a basin before the meeting. [He] unscrewed his cheeks

from a gun, laughingly gave birth to an old woman: 'Look at that! They've come!' A brunette was dying. Nikolai Vasil'evich was dying. Zhen'ka was dying and being born. A brown-haired woman was playing Chopin. But another brown-haired woman — the seventeenth — was nevertheless putting on panties . . ."[160] Whether such exercises in bizarreness are justified by the content is open to question.

An intriguing story, "You and I" strikes one as a piece of modern art (with which Tertz was well acquainted, as is testified by his co-authorship on a study of Picasso), which in its crass subjectivity precludes any unequivocal interpretation or evaluation.

e) "The Icicle" ("Gololeditsa")[161], 1961

Tertz's longest tale in the collection is, next to his novel *Liubimov,* one of his most interesting works. Unlike "You and I" with which it shares occasional excursions into formal "surrealism" (not to the detriment of content, however), it is a story singularly laden with meaning, "dense," and many-layered, bringing together many themes and motifs of Tertz's earlier tales. Combining a thin layer of apparent reality (which includes also some pungent political satire), with a rich superstructure of phantasmagoria, Tertz raises a whole series of philosophical and personal questions: the question of the uniqueness (or lack of uniqueness) of the individual, the problem of moral and aesthetic criteria, the question of death and immortality, and last but not least, the problem of the writer and literature. There is also another special feature which distinguishes "The Icicle" from the other tales: it is less morbid and hopelessly gloomy than most of them. Despite a tragic ending there seems to be a glimmer of hope in the genuine and eternal love which animates the hero for the heroine.

The story, which consists of a preface, 5 chapters, and an
epilogue, has a simple basic plot (when stripped of all philosophic
extrapolations), and is filled with suspense and quick action. It is
presented in the first person form by the narrator-hero (whose
identity remains obscure in keeping with the general thèse of the
tale) as a flashback to a crucial period in his life. The place of
action is Moscow, and the time span (excluding the preface and
the epilogue which follow about 5 years after the events of the
main part) is clearly defined: it starts on December 30, 1952, and
ends on January 19, 1953. However, unlike a similar period in
"The Trial Begins" (the last years of Stalin's rule, 1952-53), these
dates have no political implications, except for the eventual fate of
a peripheral character, colonel Tarasov, a staunch Stalinist, whose
career comes to a standstill. Rather, they refer to an icy weather
period which brings on and then ends the narrator's strange
experience, as it ends his personal happiness. This strict delineation
in time contributes to the quick action of the story, and
simultaneously seems to add a touch of irony to it — for it is
precisely the concept of time which is completely disrupted in the
course of the narrative. As already mentioned, a love story — rather
unusual for Tertz — lies at the core of the plot in "The Icicle": the
narrator who is in love with a young woman Natasha, suddenly
acquires powers of clairvoyance which permit him to see into the
past and the future. While demonstrating his ability at a New
Year's party, the hero sees his own future (a ripe old age), as well
as Natasha's (imminent death from an icicle destined to fall on her
head from a ten-story building in Gnezdnikovskii Lane at 10 a.m.,
January 19, 1953).[162] To avoid the tragedy he decides to remove
Natasha bodily from Moscow. But on the train which was to take
them to safety beyond the Ural mountains, the narrator is arrested
due to an earlier denunciation (by Natasha's husband, Boris), and
they are both returned to Moscow. And while the hero is being held

in prison and is interrogated by a zealous colonel (Tarasov) who wants to utilize his capacities for government security and for the advancement of Communism in the whole world, Natasha meets her death at the time preordained, despite his warnings. "Any accident is unavoidable, once it is predicted," the narrator reflects in the epilogue. At the moment when Natasha dies the hero inexplicably loses his mysterious abilities, and being no longer useful for the state, is returned to "normal" life.

The narrator's strange, supernatural qualities provide Tertz with an excellent opportunity to exercise his fantasy to the fullest degree. There are strange, fantastic events, visions and dreams — genuinely funny at times (with slightly satirical, political overtones), morbid, grotesque, erotically perverse at others. It is important to note also that not unlike so many earlier Romantics, Tertz tries to lend an appearance of verisimilitude to the fantastic element. His narrator is by no means an unbalanced fantast (although the question of his ultimate sanity or insanity, especially after the events described, remains open). He seems to be a perfectly normal young Soviet scientist, a materialist, and even a Marxist (even though his paraphrases of some Marxist ideas and slogans have a suspiciously-sounding naiveté). Writing retrospectively, he attributes his strange clairvoyance to a conversation about distant childhood memories with Natasha, which "served as the psychological premise for the physiological changes" that took place in him that evening. Battering "against the barriers of memory" he suddenly passes beyond them, and from that time on there are no limits to his vision into the past or the future. The first vision — a narrow ravine covered with ice, filled with a foul smell, and with a monster charging at the narrator, seems, however, to be only a grotesque transformation of the reality around him: an ice-covered Moscow boulevard, filled with the smell of gasoline, and a streetcar passing by.[163] It is only after the episode with the old ballerina

(Susanna Ivanovna) who slips on the icy ground at a spot which the narrator had instinctively predicted, and whose identy he knows without ever having seen her before, that he becomes fearfully conscious of his new ability.[164]

It becomes even more fully revealed to him at the New Year's Eve party, which forms one of the high-points of the phantas-magoric element. At first, watching the Christmas candles go out (he chooses one of them as symbol of his own life) he sees a clear and quite "realistic" picture of his own, slow death in a hospital at the age of 89. To shake off this unpleasant vision, and simul-taneously to liven up a rather dull party (made even more un-pleasant by the presence of the love-sick Boris eying Natasha) the narrator offers to predict the future of those present, without being actually quite sure that he can do it: "At first, of course, nobody believed in my talent, and I myself had my doubts. But when I began to enumerate facts, dates, and various special details from the life of the test pilot [one of the guests present] with mathe-matical speed, and he said that each time I had been correct, everybody was delighted and amazed, and interrupting each other they began to bombard me with questions."[166] While keeping at first to facts and figures, such as "date of birth, amount of salary, passport number, number of abortions" (!) he gradually notices that his vision begins to expand beyond the given individuals to their ancestors in the distant past and to their descendants in the future. The visions, contained in a matter-of-fact, sober, even quasi-scientific tone, are intended to stress, once again, the "reality" of the fantastic events. ". . . After the Georgian [who, incidentally, was an *agent provocateur* at the party, as the narrator noted], all the other guests also began somehow to change. The contours of their bodies, the outlines of their faces began to tremble, reminding one of the vibration of a signalling apparatus. Each line changed and became blurred, bringing forth tens of breathing shapes. Many of the women grew beards, blond men became dark, and then grew completely bold, then grew again new hair, then became covered with wrinkles, then grew young, so young that they looked like children — bow-legged, big-headed, dull-eyed — who in their turn began to grow, get strong, then fat, and then thin . . ."[166]

The "genealogical history" of a young engineer by the name of Bel'chikov, which is revealed to the narrator from times B.C. to the 24th century, is not only frivolously, irreverently funny, but also seems to poke fun at the Communist belief in the perfectability of human nature. One of Bel'chikov's ancestresses, as seen by the narrator, turns out bo be "a beauty, no longer quite young, but still quite serviceable — without any drapes. I, without hesitation, recognized that she was a prostitute, also probably of fairly ancient origin. With all her body she made gay signs, but my eye had no time to feast on her, when the frivolous creature disappeared, leaving instead of her either a priest, or simply an eunuch of the masculine gender . . ."[167] And when the narrator looks into Bel'chikov's future, he again sees courtesans who "developed their activities, while austere ascetics cancelled them out and expiated them," suggesting that "even in the splendid future we will not completely get rid of the dope of religion nor the frailty of women, although all this will, of course, take on new social forms and will assume a completely different appearance . . ."[168]

The second highpoint of phantasmagoria occurs after the New Year's Eve party, when the narrator experiences a similar commutation between past and future of his own personality. He sees himself as Vasilii (cf. his address to Vasilii in the preface), living in approximately the 24th century, as an Italian of the Middle Ages engaged in necrophilia, as a Red Indian swimming across a river with a scalp between his teeth, as a young boy, by the name of Mitia Diatlov, living at the beginning of the 19th century, as a dead woman (of an undefinable period), and even as prehistoric man. And while at the New Year's Eve party the narrator could calmly observe the transformation of others (e.g. those of engineer Bel'chikov — from prostitutes to priests and vice versa), now he becomes upset by the lack of system and the fragmentary quality of his visions, and by the fact that ultimately, his own identity becomes questionable: "Sometimes, in this torrent of memories flooding me I would lose my clarity of thought, as to who I was and where I was. It began to seem to me that I did not exist, and that there was only an infinite series of random episodes, which happened to other people — before me and after me. In order to reassure myself of my own authenticity I would steal up to the mirror and look at myself with great concentration. But that helped only for a short time."[169] For the mirror, he finds, does not really reflect one's real self, which remains still inside oneself, and only "pretty women ... who are not given much to thinking ... are capable of fearlessly admiring themselves for hours ..." "All the others, normal and intelligent people, cannot stand this ordeal by mirror. Because the mirror like death, is contrary to our nature, and evokes in us the same fear, distrust, and curiosity ..."[170] It is also through the mirror that the narrator has a most terrifying encounter with his most distant ancestor, prehistoric man, when his sense of identity becomes completely reversed. Looking into the mirror the narrator suddenly sees "a brown man, small, elderly, angular, who looked like a bat with folded wings," with a "bold, bony head" and "a malignant, lean face." He too was peering into a piece of crystal, and suddenly the narrator realizes that not only do they see each other simultaneously, but that he sees himself through the eyes of his ancestor: "... Who is this? Something white, slimy, perspiring. Looks like a snail. How terribly repulsive! Some kind of meat wrapped in rags. A rope [the narrator's necktie] around his neck. Must have hanged himself. A degenerate."[171]

There are other, minor fantastic events, as e.g. on the train to Siberia, when the narrator becomes conscious of all his ancestors residing simultaneously within himself (with the actual result that he eats a lot, dividing the food between his various "selves" — Mitia Diatlov being his special favorite), when he "sees" the secret police searching the train for him before they actually appear, when his various "selves" give him different advices how to act in this moment of danger: "Some — probably former women — told me to leave Natasha as soon as possible ('why get involved with such trash, save yourself before it is too late!'). Others were mostly worried about the money spent, which had to be returned within a month. And someone adviced to offer armed resistance"[172] Finally, perhaps the narrator's prophetic dream in prison should be mentioned, when he sees himself as Vasilii (in the 24th century) going to visit Natasha, and being shot by a road patrol (the totalitarian conditions of life in the Soviet Union apparently having changed but little!). He nevertheless reaches her house and sees her through a window reading his book (*this* book which he is writing in the 20th century), but although he knocks at the window she cannot hear him since he is already dead.

The whole complex of ideas which underlies this phantasmagoria are, as already mentioned, the "eternal" problems of death, immortality, personal identity, and moral and aesthetic criteria. These questions, especially the question of death and immortality in the face of religious disbelief, had already cropped up on the periphery of some of Tertz's earlier stories. Karlinskii (in "The Trial Begins") had tried to fill the fearful void by a Purpose (Marina), Kostia (in "At the Circus") by his striving for a marvellous "trick". Even Straustin's graphomania ("The Graphomaniacs") was partially a striving for immortality. In "The Icicle" the narrator returns time and again to the problem of death, which requires one's disassociation from one's self (it is like looking at

oneself in a mirror, only "ten times worse"), and which is unavoidable, and unpredictable (under normal circumstances). "I do not
consider myself a pessimist," the narrator says at one point, "but
I must say with all due sense of responsibility that, if you penetrate
deeply into the essence of life, it becomes clear that everything ends
in death . . ." "All this would not be too bad," he continues, making
an obvious (and ironic) allusion to Marx's theories of history, "if
there were full equality, brotherhood, and iron laws in this matter.
If, e.g. we would depart from the face of earth in an organized
manner, in large collectives, by series, e.g. according to age group
or nationality. One nation has lived its set period, and that's it,
let's have the next. — Then everything would be, of course, simpler
and the inevitability of this separation would not have such agitat-
ing and nerve-racking sharpness . . ."[173]

Since the narrator does not believe in any non-materialistic
theory or religion (there is no soul, he argues, but only "openings
in the air, and through these openings passes a nervous current of
separate psychic conditions, which change from instance to instance,
from epoch to epoch"),[174] he tries to find another path to immortality. His strange visions confirm in him a belief in a physical,
tangible carry-over of physical and psychological features from
generation to generation. Throughout the story, he tries to find
additional scientific "proofs" for his theory of reincarnation of
matter. Thus on the train he seems to discern the outlines of
prehistorical tropical vegetation in the icecovered trees of the
Russian landscape; he remembers that the human embryo in its
initial state has the shape of a fish,[175] and comes to the conclusion
that "all is rooted in one another, reflected, solidified," and that
"nothing perishes in nature . . ." He even finds rather interesting
proofs for his theory in various deviations from the norm, among
the physically deformed, and the mad, which deserve to be quoted
in full: "Let's take the obvious example of children born with six

fingers," the narrator muses. "A child is born, and instead of 5 fingers he has 6. The question is: where did the extra finger come from? Medicine is helpless. But if you think about it and use your brain, it becomes clear that it is he, the stranger, the hidden one, who has long since died, who decided to make himself known, and making use of a propitious moment, shoved an additional finger through somebody's palm. As if to say: 'Here I am! Here, I sit here and am bored, and would like to at least wiggle my little finger an God's earth.'"[176] As regards the madmen, the narrator says: "[A man] walks around haughtily and tells everyone: 'I am Julius Caesar.' And nobody believes him. Nobody but me. I believe him because I know: he was Julius Caesar. Well, perhaps not Caesar himself, but some other, also outstanding military leader. He only forgot a little who he was, when, which branch of the army . . ."[177] Apart from the fact that these "proofs" raise the question of the narrator's own sanity, their naive (though consistent) logic renders the whole theory ridiculous, and provides an excellent example of Tertz's love for ambiguity and "double-talk."

This materialistic theory of reincarnation raises, quite obviously, a moral question: the problem of personal identity and personal responsibility for one's action. After seeing human outlines (and characteristics) wave and blur at the New Year's Eve party, the narrator comes to the conclusion that one has no right to say "He is a thief" and "I am an engineer," because "there is basically no 'I' or 'he,' and we all are thieves and prostitutes and perhaps even worse. And if you think that you are not, then you were temporarily lucky, but in the past, even if it were a thousand years ago, we were all like that, or inevitably will be that in the future, as our sweet memories and bitter forebodings keep telling."[178] Another, cleverly manipulated idea from Marx (ostensibly to reinforce the narrator's viewpoint) further complements his deterministic ideas: "I know well," the narrator says, "that each person,

even if he were Leonardo da Vinci himself, is the product of
economical forces, which produce and economize everything in this
world . . ."[179] "And what kind of independence can a man have,"
he says in prison, in an intentionally ambiguous situation, "when
everything is taken into consideration? Get up! — I get up. Lie
down! — I lie down. I don't want to, but have to. Because it is the
law, historical necessity . . ."[180] Thus if man is the product of a
given society and its economics, and in addition, a tangible carry-
over of his ancestors, then the question of free will and personal
responsibility does not arise at all. Furthermore, morality itself
becomes irrelevant (cf. Bel'chikov's prostitutes and priests, the
narrator's necrophilia incident), and even aesthetic criteria are no
longer valid (cf. the narrator's encounter with his prehistorical
ancestor). Man has been reduced to a semi-mechanical, predictable
"piano key," to use Dostoevskii's terminology.

Yet it seems that Tertz who is echoing some of the problems
raised by Dostoevskii in "Notes from Underground" had presented
the materialistic, rational arguments only to reduce them *ad
absurdum*. Besides, there is a dangerously weak spot in the narrator's system of rationality and belief in matter because of his
completely irrational, and intensely personal love for Natasha.
Natasha is Tertz's only lovable female character, "positive" not so
much by virtue of her personality or action, but rather by the
feelings which she inspires in the narrator. She is a rather ordinary,
educated Soviet young woman who is studying at the university
(writing a dissertation on Turgenev). Since her husband Boris
won't agree to a divorce, she divides her favors between him ("out
of pity and force of habit"), and the narrator ("out of love").
Eventually she even gets pregnant without knowing to whom to
attribute the paternity of her future child. But Natasha's
"weakness" which becomes apparent to the narrator after he
acquires his powers of clairvoyance, does not change anything in

his feelings for her. He loves her for what she is for him, his "untouched, eternal, only, and indivisible Natasha," and even more so because of the danger that threatens her. He tries to save her, warns her not to go to Gnezdnikovskii Lane (which she nevertheless does), he dreams of her while being in prison, and he ends his story (after her death) with an anguished outcry, a desperate reaching into the beyond: "I tell you, Natasha, before the end comes. Wait one second. The story is not finished. I want to say something to you. The last thing that I have the strength to say ... Natasha, I love you. I love you, Natasha. I love you so much, so much ..."[181] Thus one of the main impulses for the narrator's belief in reincarnation seems to be love, and faith in love as absolute, invariable, eternal. And one of his purposes in telling the story is, as he states in the preface, to be read by Vasilii (his future reincarnation) and to be reunited with Natasha (in her new reincarnation), in order to find the happiness which he had missed in the previous existence.

Of all the narrator's in the "Fantastic Tales," the anonymous narrator in "The Icicle" seems closest to Tertz in his preoccupation with death (cf. "Thoughts at Random"), his groping for immortality, his feeling of isolation ("... he [Vasilii] like me, is lost in the waves of time and space," he says in the introduction), but most of all through the motif of literature which is stressed toward the end of the story, and by the various literary allusions that occur throughout the tale, and which do not quite fit the image of the narrator-scientist. World literature, the narrator finds, is both a struggle with death, and a path to immortality: "I am sure: most books are letters thrown into the future with a reminder of that which happened ... They are attempts at re-establishing, retrospectively, one's relation with oneself as well as one's former relatives and friends who live on and do not remember that they are missing persons (propavshie bez vesti)."[182] His last words, addressed to the future Natasha reading this book, is also an attempt to penetrate into the future: "And I write from here, I write, trying to penetrate there [into the future], and I do not know whether I will ever hear this forlorn tapping . . ."[183] The literary allusions are, at times quite funny, and range from Pushkin ("an ancient Russian writer" who "was shot 500 years ago," the narrator as Vasilii explains to his wife in the 24th century) to Boldyrev ("another famous writer" who "was shot 200 years ago"). There are also quotes from Pushkin (cf. the poem "Do not sing, o beautiful maiden, in my presence." /"Ne poi, krasavitsa, pri mne"), and a very obvious paraphrase of Gogol' 's famous digression on the troika at the end of *Dead Souls*, applied to a contemporary vehicle, the train:

"Oh you train, train like a bird! Who has invented you? It's certain that you could have been born only of a quickwitted people! And although no artful peasant of Tula or Iaroslavl' has invented you, but a clever Englishman [by the name of] Stephenson, as they say, for the general good, still you are mightily well fitted for our Russian plains, and you dash on along mounds and hills, past telephone poles, now slowing down, now going faster until one gets dizzy. But if one looks closer, it [the train] is nothing but a stove on wheels, a village samovar with something hooked on to it. An angry creature at first sight, but kind, magnanimous, curly-haired . . ."[184]

Finally, a pseudo-Romantic passage in the preface, in which the narrator compares himself to a castaway trying to send a message to the inhabited world, is interesting not only as an example for the ecclecticism of Tertz's style. It seems also to be a subtle allusion to Tertz's own feelings, and to his captive position as a writer in the Soviet Union:

"I write this tale as a castaway tells of his distress. Sitting on a lonely piece of wreckage or on an uninhabited island, he throws a bottle with a letter into the stormy ocean — in the hope that the waves and the wind will carry it to people, and that they will read it and learn the sad truth, at a time when the poor author is no longer alive.

Will the bottle reach land? That is the question. Will the sinewy arm of a sailor haul it out by the neck, and will the sailor shed tears of sympathy and pity onto the deck of his ship? Or will sea salt gradually impregnate the sealing wax, and eat away the paper, and the unknown bottle, filled with bitter sea water or broken against the reefs, will remain motionless on the bottom of the sea?"[185]

But "The Icicle" is not only a sad tale, filled with complex philosophical ideas and personal thoughts of its author. At times it is simply and irresistibly funny. as e.g., in the episode in prison (chapter 5) where the narrator is interrogated by colonel Tarasov, a naive and zealous Communist, somewhat reminiscent of the Public Prosecutor Globov in "The Trial Begins." Colonel Tarasov is not content to know the course of history in advance; he is anxious to "improve" on it, and to hasten the advance of Communism throughout the world ... In a hilarious scene, Tarasov is presented pouring over a geographical map, trying to "introduce clarity into the international position" by invading Australia:

" 'Are you mad?' " the narrator tries to restrain him. " 'First of all, we are not here, but there. Take away your finger. Also, colonel, you forget Madagascar. The Japanese are there. Where are you pointing at? We can't go there. We'll lose the campaign. We can't, I tell you. In the final analysis, I know better what will happen ...'

He looked at me with tearful eyes and said hoarsely: 'And how about Australia?'

'What does Australia have to do with it?'

'Do you mean we'll let Australia go to the dogs?'

'Well, you know, you can't have everything at once. At some time, when there will be another vacancy, it will be Australia's turn. At a higher stage of the historical development...' The colonel crawled on his elbows across the table toward me:

'Old chap, couldn't it be speeded up? Even a little ...'

'Speed up what?'

'Well, that very development ... Why bother about it so long! Try! Well, for my sake, for friendship's sake. I ask you as a friend, be a decent man, help out Australia ...'

It seems he confused me with the Lord God."[186]

The formal composition and style of "The Icicle" reflects, to some degree, the complexity of its ideas. Apart from the strange visions and dreams already described, Tertz uses also his "surrealist" technique, in which events and objects are disjointed and put together in wrong order (cf. "You and I"). This is especially prominent in chapter 3, which deals with the narrator's strange commutation between past and future, and where the logic of time and space are completely disrupted.

"The woodcock dropped dead from the birch tree, as if pulled by a string. I pressed the trigger, and taking aim, I saw that it was sitting on a branch, a big black cock, and was looking at Diana. We got off our horses and gallopped away. 'Hunter's luck!' Katen'ka in a pink negligé waves goodbye from the veranda. Jumping into the saddle I ran down the porch and pulled on my boots. 'It's time to get up, master, it will soon be daybreak,' Nikifor shouts into my ear. My hands clasped his strong calves. 'Don't leave us, for God's sake, I implore you for the sake of your son ...' He looks away, pale with anger: 'Someone may see us, madam.' I took the scalp between my teeth and began to swim. In the middle of the river I felt faint. Without unclinching my teeth I began to sink ..."[187] In this passage, not only is a hunting episode shown in reverse order (like a movie being shown backwards), but the narrator's personality of a Russian squire is suddenly transformed into that of a woman, and then into a Red Indian.

Similarly, Mitia Diatlov's sneezing is shown in a kind of cinemascopic vision — with strange actions taking place simultaneously in various parts of the world:

"He sneezed once — there was a landslide in the Himalayas, the fragments of the sky buried us together with our stretchers.

He sneezed a second time — lightning struck the church of the Holy Trinity, it thundered, the roof of the barn started to burn, haystacks were burning.

He sneezed a third time — there was a flood, pastor Zinovii Shvarts mounted on a cow ferried chairs in their covers . . ."[188]

But more interesting than this formal experimentation is the symbol of the icicle and ice-covered ground that runs through the tale. It refers not only to the time period of the plot, delineated by the narrator's first vision (an ice-covered ravine) and his last one (again, a glacial landscape); it seems also to suggest a certain cyclic repetition of historical periods: ice at the beginning of time, ice again in the future, rather than continuous progress of humanity, a "golden age" of Communism. Perhaps there is also some significance in the fact that Natasha is killed by an icicle (a fact which could, perhaps, have been avoided, had colonel Tarasov not been so fearful of overstepping "Soviet legality" in arresting her, as the narrator had requested), and that in the last vision Tarasov appears to the narrator in the shape of a huge icicle: ". . . The icicle closest to me, which seemed to rule the whole landscape, was nothing else but colonel Tarasov, except that now he had a different rank, and probably another name, and little resembled his previous appearance. However, in the very structure, and the way of life of this icy polypus — who, . . . was continuously growing, and developing, and while developing, he attacked with powerful spikes his neighboring formations — in all this, I say, I felt the former persistence and statesmanship of colonel Tarasov, and even some kind of internal honesty and straightforwardness . . ."[189] Perhaps the title of the tale is Tertz's answer to Erenburg's *Thaw*, which was written at a time when there was hope for a rebirth of freedom. By 1961 the "thaw" had turned to cold, to ice, and ice-covered ground. Hardly any other tale by Tertz is so deeply laden with meaning as "The Icicle."

f) "Pkhents"

Tertz's last story to reach the West is in some ways a unique performance among his fantastic tales. Although it is relatively simple and short, requiring no special "key" to be understood, still it is a compact tale — basically sad, yet at times grotesquely funny, — filled with philosophical and psychological observation and poignant character studies. In its plotless structure, "open" end, and first person diary form, "Pkhents" is somewhat reminiscent of "The Graphomaniacs", with which it also shares an abrupt beginning *in medias res*. Yes despite a wealth of realistic and even naturalistic details (cf. the first scene in which the narrator watches a hunchback deliver his soiled wash to a laundry), as well as some veiled (but obvious) autobiographical elements, the story is based on a fantastic premise of the H. G. Wells science-fiction type:[190] the presence of a being from another planet in present-day society, in this case Soviet Russia.

Living in a Moscow communal apartment, the narrator-hero passes for Andrei Kazimirovich Sushinskii, an elderly (61 years old) book-keeper, "half-Polish, half Russian by nationality, an invalid [seemingly a hunchback], not a Party member, single." But in reality he is a being from another planet, who had the misfortune of crashing in Siberia some time in the 1920's, and who subsequently assumed the guise of man. ". . . We were not about to fly into any space," the narrator recapitulates the catastrophe, "but, to put it simply, we were just going to a holiday resort. But on the way, something happened — let's say it was a meteorite, to make it easier for you, — and we fell, losing our connection, into the unknown, we fell for seven and a half months (but our months, not yours), and as a result of pure chance we landed here."[191] Finding his fellow-travellers dead, the hero made his way to people, assumed their appearance as much as he could, and even studied their language and sciences (for a time teaching arithmetics in a high school in Irkutsk!), ending up as a book-keeper in an unidentified office in Moscow. Yet even after 32 years of life on earth, he still remains alien to humanity, is beset by nostalgia for his lost homeland, loneliness, and fear of being discovered. In order to preserve his secret (which, at one point is threatened by a girl who falls in love with him), he decides to leave Moscow and to return to Siberia, to die there in peace: ". . . And when the first frosts come, and I'll see that the time has come, then just one match will be enough. Nothing will be left [of me]."[192]

The hero's "estranged" vision of human life and mores (which is revealed only gradually, to build up suspense about his identity), provides Tertz with a splendid opportunity for debunking humanity, by pointing to the "low," revolting aspects of man (e.g. his natural functions, food, sex) and by showing the relativity of his moral and aesthetic criteria.

The habit of man to consume food fills Andrei Kazimirovich with revulsion. For although masquerading as a human being with the aid of various contraptions (e.g. strapping his extra arms to his back in the form of a hump, putting on a wig, guttapercha ears, and face powder), he is in reality a cactus-type organism who needs only water for sustenance: ". . . The sadism of cooking always amazed me. Would be chicken are being consumed in liquid form. The entrails of pigs are stuffed with their own meat. A gut which has swallowed itself and over which stillborn chicken are poured — this is what actually scrambled eggs and sausage are." His thoughts wander on, to a grotesque analogy applied to humans: "What if one were to prepare man according to the same recipe? Take some engineer or writer, stuff him with his own brains, place a violet in one braised nostril, and dish him up to his colleagues for dinner? No, the torments of Christ, Jan Hus, and Sten'ka Razin are nothing compared to the agonies of a fish pulled out of the water on a hook. They at least knew what it was all for."[193]

Even less comprehensible to Andrei Kazimirovich is the mystery which surrounds the human body. "... A kick is ... considered a more insulting action than a blow with the hand, and not only because the foot can hurt more. Probably this inequality is due to the persistence of Christianity. The foot must be more sinful than the rest of the body for the simple reason that it is farther removed from heaven. Only the sexual organs are treated even worse, and here there is some mystery."[194] When Veronika, Andrei Kazimirovich's only friend in the otherwise hostile communal apartment professes her love and offers her body to him, Andrei Kazimirovich (after taking a close look at it) flees in disgust. This detailed description of a naked feminine body is a marvellous example of "estrangement" on Tertz's part, and a good example of morbid eroticism:

"It was — I repeat — horrible. It turned out that her whole body was of the same unnatural whiteness as her neck, face and hands. In front, a pair of white breasts was dangling. At first I took them for a pair of secondary arms amputated above the elbow. But each of them terminated in a round nipple which looked like a push-button.

And farther on — up to her very legs — the whole available space was taken up by a spherical belly. Here all the food swallowed in the course of the day collects into a single heap. Its lower part was covered with curly hair like a head . . ." Taking a closer look at Veronika's "childbearing apparatus" (he had studied it only in textbooks on anatomy before) Andrei Kazimirovich notices something resembling "a man's face, elderly, unshaven, with bared teeth." He concludes that "a hungry,, angry man dwelt there between her legs. He probably snored at night and used foul language from boredom. Probably this explains the duality of woman's nature, of which the poet Lermontov so aptly said: 'Fair as an angel of heaven, as a demon crafty and wicked . . .'"[195]

Andrei Kazimirovich's revulsion at the sight of Veronika's body reflects the inapplicability of traditional human aesthetic values to a creature from another world.[196] At the same time, it also seems to reflect Tertz's interest in modern art, which reverses the classical concept of beauty. To Andrei Kazimirovich, human beings are indescribably ugly, and if he were one, he says at one point, he would "not get out of a fur coat, let alone a suit, day or night . . ." Even more, he would undergo "a plastic operation, so that the legs would be shorter, and there would be at least a hump on the back. Hunchbacks here are still a little betterlooking than the rest of them, although they too are ugly . . ."[197] This "different" aesthetic concept leads Andrei Kazimirovich to follow another hunchback ("graceful, bent, unlike a human being"), whom he suspects to be also a cactus in disguise, but who turns out to be only a human hunchback.

Ideal harmonious beauty, according to Andrei Kazimirovich, does not exist on this earth. It exists only in his long lost homeland, in his beautiful, nearly forgotten language (of which he remembers only a few words, such as the sacred word "Pkhents"), and his own body: "Let my rear arm be twisted from the constant necessity of having to represent a human hump. Let two fingers of my front arm, maimed by straps, be withered, let my old body lose its former suppleness! Nevertheless, I am beautiful! Proportionate! Elegant! No matter what enviers and crittlers may say."[198]

Being conscious of his uniqueness, he is at the same time aware of the danger which his "strangeness" bears for him, of being discovered and persecuted (a rather frequent motif in Tertz's stories): "... They would consider me a madman, a fantast, and even more, they might put me on trial for having a false passport, forging signatures and stamps, and for other illegal activities."[199] But even if his fantastic story were to be believed, he visualizes his future as a "celebrity" with horror, with dissertations, movies and poems about him circulating in millions, and "ladies painting their lips with green lipstick and ordering hats in the shape of a cactus or at least, a rubber plant . . ."[200] And after his death he sees himself being pickled in alcohol and put in a big glass jar on exhibit in a zoological museum as a freak of nature.

To escape such fate and to preserve his dignity and the secret of his mysterious country of origin, Andrei Kazimirovich wants to disappear into the unknown as he had come. The paradox, however, is that despite his longing for his homeland, he has also acquired some human habits and traits, and that in consequence, he seems to belong nowhere. "Strange desires come upon me at times. Now I feel like going to the movies. Now I feel like playing checkers with Veronika Grigor'evna's husband [Veronika having married after her "disappointment" over Andrei Kazimirovich] . . . It is getting harder and harder for me to remember the past. Only a few words of my native language have been preserved. I even can no longer think in my language, not to speak of writing and speaking. I remember something beautiful, but what — I don't know . . ."[201] He closes his diary with the few words which he still remembers from the past: "Gogry! Gogry! Tuzheroskip. Pkhents . .."[202] This feeling of alienation, of not belonging anywhere is perhaps also a reflection of the feelings and fate of Tertz himself.

But "Pkhents" is not only a somber, symbolic tale of loneliness and alienation. It has, at times, some quite realistic and funny
incidents and descriptions, such as the hero's secret nocturnal visits
to the communal bathroom where he "eats" by pouring water over
his parched cactus-body. Andrei Kazimirovich's difficult rela-
tionship with Veronika is also occasionally quite comical. "You
remind me of a cactus," she says quite innocently during a dinner,
while he tries discreetly to get rid of the food which she puts before
him. When during an illness he becomes completely dried out and
is literally dying for water, Veronika (with a full bottle of water
in her hand) goes off on a lengthy monologue analyzing her former
feelings for him: ". . . I loved you really, Andrei Kazimirovich. I
understand: this was a love — how to explain to you? — love out
of pity . . . Pity for a lonely, deformed man, forgive my frankness.
But I began to pity you so much . . . not to notice . . . physical
defects. You seemed to me, Andrei Kazimirovich, the most handsome human being on earth . . . man himself. And when you so
cruelly laughed . . . Commit suicide . . . I loved . . . I won't conceal
and will say . . . a worthy man . . . I have fallen in love again . . .
And now I am even grateful . . . I have fallen in love . . . with a
man . . . human . . . humanity . . . as a human being to a human
being . . ."[203]

The description of the atmosphere of Leonid Sergeevich's (the
real hunchback's) communal apartment is a sketchy, but masterful
portrayal of Soviet *byt*: starting with the fat, perfume-reeking
landlady, her querulous child (by Leonid Sergeevich, as it turns out),
and ending with the other gossiping inhabitants (who start
discussing the ugly visitor as soon as he appears, not realizing his
heightened sense of hearing), and a vicious dog trying to get his
teeth into Andrei Kazimirovich's cactus-body. The ensuing conversation between the two hunchbacks, based on false premises on
Andrei Kazimirovich's part, is grotesquely funny. "Pkhents!

Pkhents!" the hero repeats to Leonid Sergeevich, shaking him by
the shoulders, in order to make him remember his native language.
Suddenly, however, he feels warmth reaching him through Leonid
Sergeevich's jacket: "... His shoulders were getting hotter and
hotter, just as hot as Veronika's hand, like thousands of other hot
hands which I chose not to shake in greeting. 'Forgive me,' I said,
and relaxed my grip. 'It seems there is a mistake. A regrettable
misunderstanding, you see — how can I explain it to you — I am
subject to nervous attacks . . .' "[204]

Even if the theme of "Pkhents" — the loneliness and isolation
of a "different" individual — is hardly new and original, Tertz's
handling of it is powerful, concise, and memorable in its fantastic
"realness."

4. *Liubimov*[205] *(The Makepeace Experiment)*, 1961—62

Tertz's last fictional work, the novel *Liubimov*, can be said
to represent a summary of Tertz's philosophical and artistic ideas.
The question of the development of history, of Purpose, of ends
and means, which Tertz had raised in his essay on socialist realism,
and which underlay the plot of "The Trial Begins," are now
incorporated in the "history" of the fictional Russian provincial
town of Liubimov. *Liubimov* is both a political satire, and a
timeless anti-Utopia. In contrast to the earlier story, "The Trial
Begins," however, the philosophical and literary elements dominate
by far over the political.[206] In this *Liubimov* resembles "The Icicle"
(written at approximately the same time), with which it also shares
the motifs of supernatural powers mysteriously acquired by the
respective heroes (in this instance, they *do* influence and regulate
events), as well as of spiritual "transmigration" between past and
present. Futhermore, the basic philosophical problem that underlies
the plot of *Liubimov* is, as in "The Icicle," the Dostoevskian juxta-

position of man's freedom of will and his right to irrationality versus regulated, rational "happiness."

In terms of Tertz's literary theory, *Liubimov* is a perfect example of phantasmagoria, and of Tertz's non-realistic, dense, ornamental style. It abounds in literary associations and parody (Saltykov-Shchedrin's *History of a Town /Istoriia odnogo goroda*, being one of the most obvious models), grotesque humor, irony, and shifts in time and narrative voice. *Liubimov* is certainly Tertz's most complex and best work, and least amenable to one, definite interpretation. It sparkles like a many-faceted jewel, and each shift in viewpoint brings out another, different aspect in it.

The novel is presented as the ostensible Chronicle of the small town of Liubimov, recorded by its elderly, semi-educated librarian, Savelii Kuzmich Proferansov. It consists of a preface, which provides a sketchy background of the narrator, and some rather comical descriptions of the city and its recent past. This is followed by the main part (chapters 1-6), which describes the "scientific revolution" carried out on May 1, 1958 by the young bicycle repairman Lenia Tikhomirov in the town of Liubimov, which fundamentally (although only temporarily) alters the lives of all its inhabitants. The final, 7th chapter, which takes place a few months later (its latter part is dated about a year after the initial events) tells of the fates of the respective main protagonists, Lenia Tikhomirov and Savelii Kuzmich, after the revolution had misfired.

The plot of *Liubimov* is somewhat reminiscent of the plot of "The Icicle" in appearing also as a "concurrence of anecdotal circumstances," mixed with a goodly amount of phantasmagoria, and with a love story (though grotesque and one-sided) providing the impetus for the action: If Serafima Petrovna had not spurned Lenia's love . . . If Lenia had not started to improve his mind by reading . . . If a book on magic had not fallen into his hands — there would be no story of Liubimov.

Lenia Tikhomirov, a simple young man, though an indus-
trious and inventive bicycle repairman, falls madly in love with
a *femme fatale*, Serafima Petrovna Kozlova, a school teacher from
Leningrad. She had already managed to turn the heads of most of
the male population of the town (including even that of the
chronicler, Savelii Kuzmich) by her city manners, apparent
haughtiness, and a luxurious bosom which she likes to display.
When Lenia declares his love for her, she rejects him as unworthy
of her, demanding of him some heroic deed, such as the city of
Liubimov to be placed at her feet, "just to start with." Upon the
advice of Savelii Kuzmich (who overhears this conversation which
takes place in the library) Lenia tries to drown his grief in reading:
"—A book is like a bottle of five-star brandy: you finish one, you
want the next."[207] After having gone through books on such
different "great" men as Copernicus, Napoleon, Chapaev, and Don
Quixote, Lenia turns to scientific works. He begins to study various
treatises on the nervous system, on magnetic physics and psychology
(not forgetting such solidly "orthodox" works as Engels's *Dialectics
of Nature*), when suddenly an old book entitled *The Magnet of the
Soul (Psikhicheskii magnit)* falls literally from the ceiling of his
home into his hands. This book, an apparent relic from a common
ancestor of Lenia and Savelii Kuzmich, Samson Samsonovich
Proferansov, a rich gentleman who lived in the 19th century and
had dabbled in magic and all sorts of psychic sciences, turns out
to be the final impulse in Lenia's aspiration to greatness and his
formulation of a new theory. Having read in Engels that "consciousness is the highest product of matter," and that as such it is
subject to change, Lenia conceives the grandiose idea of changing
the consciousness of the inhabitants of Liubimov by instilling in
them the "proper" way of thought: respect for work, love of the
fatherland, and the desire to continually elevate their material
and cultural level. This idea is first applied during the May Day

celebration in Liubimov: by an effort of his will, Lenia forces the
city Party secretary to abdicate "voluntarily" from his post, and
to nominate Lenia "supreme leader, judge, commander in chief."
After having been unanimously accepted by the populace, Lenia
declares Liubimov a free city, which guarantees "freedom and
autonomy to all its citizens," and sends telegrams to that effect
to the rest of the country.

The high-point of Lenia's triumph occurs a few days later
(chapter 3), when Lenia celebrates his marriage to Serafima
Petrovna, who has now fallen madly in love with him. Making
the celebration an occasion for a popular feast, Lenia demonstrates
his powers and good will to the citizens of Liubimov. Since the
food reserves of the city are minimal, Lenia resorts to mass
hypnotism, suggesting that mineral water is vodka, cucumbers are
sausage, and red peppers are beef (it's only the dogs of Liubimov
who refuse to eat it!). Finally, he makes the local stream flow
champagne for half an hour: "[Champagne] of the highest quality.
'Soviet Champagne' . . . Don't be afraid, it's a new achievement of
technology . . . Go and drink! Stop! Not all at once! You will crush
each other, you brutes! Children are forbidden to drink! Invalids
are to have priority! Use glasses. Don't wade in with your feet, or
else you will drown . . ."[208] Lenia issues his orders.

The day is marred, however, by two incidents. One is the
death of one man (an amnestied thief from prison) who dies,
ironically, from an overdose of Lenia's "vodka." The other is the
appearance of enemy forces (a detachment of soldiers under the
leadership of colonel Almazov from the city of N.) to crush the
revolution in Liubimov. And while Lenia does not resurrect the
dead man, despite Serafima's desire to witness a miracle, he does
disperse the enemy by an effort of his will: their trucks break down,
they get lost in the swampy area surrounding Liubimov (which
disappears from sight as if swallowed from the face of the earth),

and partly scared, partly hypnotized by the presence of some
supernatural being, the colonel and his "army" beat a retreat.[209]

The building of a new, better society proves, however, to be
a tougher job than Lenia had envisaged. And although he wins a
loyal friend in the person of an enemy — the secret agent Vitalii
Kochetov, who had figured in "The Trial Begins,"[210] sent from
Moscow to investigate the "revolution," but whose consciousness
becomes duly transformed — Lenia becomes disappointed in his
subjects as well as his wife. When bad weather hits the area the
peasants begin to grumble, demanding that he stop the rain (which
he cannot do), complaining of the quality of vodka (rationed, to
prevent further deaths) which does not give them a proper hang-
over, and showing in general, complete "lack of ideology." When
the rumor that "the Czar is a magician, and the Czarina a Jewess"
reaches Lenia, and he begins to inquire into the background of his
consort, he discovers to his consternation that Serafima is indeed
partly Jewish (her maiden name having been Fisher); but worse
than that he finds out that she had been married previously, had
born a child, and had had love affairs with half a dozen men,
including colonel Almazov (from the town of N), and Dr. Linde
(from Liubimov). But the greatest blow to Lenia is the realization
that he is beginning to lose his hypnotic powers, and that they are
not really his, but have been "lent" to him temporarily by his
ancestor Samson Samsonovich Proferansov, who engages him in a
nocturnal, nightmarish conversation (chapter 4). Although Lenia
still manages to ward off an airplane attack, ordered by Moscow,
from the city, he begins to lose ground: Part of the population
begins to desert Liubimov, Serafima Petrovna escapes with a big
sum of money — for Lenia had papered his study with bank-notes
in his attempt to abolish the monetary system. The magic book
mysteriously disappears from the safe. Although at the very end
Lenia has a short return of will power which results in some

grotesque episodes, his experiment has failed. He cannot ward off an attack by unmanned amphibious tanks which enter Liubimov from all sides. The only defender of the city, Vitia Kochetov, is killed, while Lenia escapes on the next freight train leaving for distant Russian provinces. The *status quo* is restored, the former city Party secretary returns to power, and Savelii Kuzmich, the official historiographer of Liubimov, is seen trembling in fear over the fate of his "heretical" Chronicle.

Tertz's satire in *Liubimov* moves on two levels — a direct, topical (political) connected with the many incongruities of Soviet *byt*, and a more complex historical, philosophical which ties it to Tertz's weltanschauung. Tertz's portrayal of Soviet totalitarian society brings out strikingly the difference between leadership and the masses: the attempts of the former at politicizing all spheres of life, at strict adherence to dogma, at cultivation of personality "cults" are met with a completely intransigent political apathy on the part of the population. Although the place of action in the novel is present-day Soviet Russia, Communism seems to be a formality rather than a way of life in Liubimov. It is not for nothing that Lenia Tikhomirov decides to improve on it, and to translate its ideals once more into practice. And it is rather ironic that while to some citizens of Liubimov Lenia seems to be a new Czar (a good one as long as he satisfies their wishes, and a bad one when he fails to do so), and to others, mostly women, a saint, a messenger of God, the *ideological* background of his rule is of absolutely no interest to them.

One of the best examples of this topical satire is the description of the May Day Celebration (chapter 1), which strikingly emphasizes the contrast between an official, obligatory enthusiasm, and the sad reality of a small, politically apathetic provincial town: "The whole space has been cleaned, puddles have been filled, and not a single cow or even a sheep nibbling the young grass can be seen.

On top of the watch-tower a red banner flutters proudly while
below a row of militiamen made up of five individuals — the
whole garrison — keep a sharp lookout in order to prevent the
infiltration of premature drunkards on the square, who by their
lax appearance could spoil the international demonstration . . ."[211]

The events leading to Lenia's elevation — Tishchenko's voluntary resignation, his nomination of Lenia, the latter's "unanimous"
acceptance by the populace who immediately rejects its former
leader — are not only satirical descriptions of Soviet political
reality, but also seem to symbolize Soviet history in miniature:
"Dear fellow citizens," Tishchenko suddenly announces, "dear
fellow citizens . . . I wish . . . we wish . . . to announce . . . from this
day on . . . from this day on a new era starts in Liubimov. The
whole leadership, with me at its head, voluntarily — I underline
this! — voluntarily divests itself of all its functions. To fill the
vacancy, I immediately order the confirmation, through universal
election, of one man who will lead us . . . our pride . . . our glory . . .
I order . . . I beg . . ."[212] When Tishchenko, gurgling, stumbling over
words, and looking like "a crab with his claws spread out to the
sides" (under the influence of Lenia's hypnotic powers) proposes
the election of Leonid Ivanovich Tikhomirov as the new leader,
the population reacts with typical, politically conditioned reflexes
of obedience. "At first the people were silent,"[213] while only the
teeth of comrade Mariamov (the chief of the secret police who had
most reasons to fear any political changes) were audibly chattering.
But half a minute later, the crowd showed its approval by loudly
hailing the new leader: "Long live Tikhomirov! Glory to Leonid
Ivanovich!"

When a peasant starts asking his fellow-citizens as to who this
Tikhomirov was and why he was being elected, this "ignoramus"
is immediately put down and silenced. "No one considered it
strange that the bicycle repairman Lenia, a youth who had been

completely unknown yesterday, had risen to such heights in one moment. On the contrary, everyone was amazed that Leonid Ivanovich had not been offered some leading position in Liubimov until now, and that our brainless town administration had dared to disregard his organizational talent!"[214] And while his predecessor, Tishchenko, is heaped with abuse, a final satirical touch to Lenia's meteoric rise to power is added by a miracle: a two months old baby that had been brought by its mother to the celebration, "woke up, got out of its swaddling clothes, bared his toothless gums from ear to ear, and began to squeal: 'I want,' he said, 'I demand that Lenia Tikhomirov should be Czar in our town!' Thunderous applause drowned out his childish prattle."[215]

Another example of extremely funny political satire are the descriptions of the political bosses of N and their reactions to the news of Lenia's take-over of Liubimov (chapter 3). Comrade O, "completely bald," with "smiling blue eyes," uneducated and ruthless (a partial take-off on Khrushchev, as Siniavskii himself admitted), is the real boss, even though he pretends to be only a *primus inter pares*. Comrade U, his closest colleague, rarely utters a word, and carries his solidarity with comrade O to the point of shaving off his hair, despite the fact that this considerably lessens his chances for "closer contact with the female population of the town of N." Finally, there is lieutenant colonel Almazov, a remnant from the *ancien régime*, who hides his gentry origin, without being able to overcome his gentlemanly predilection for women, elegant living (on his campaign against Liubimov he carries with him a fragrant towel and a silver soap dish), and hunting. The secret telephone code invented by him is composed of hunting terms and pure nonsense: "In Liubimov the mating (tokovanie) of bears has begun," the lieutenant on duty informs Almazov about the Liubimov revolution. "The bear twitters in Calmuck. Time to slit its throat. Drowned corpse arrived by sledge, injection required . . ."[216]

The "corpse," incidentally, is the same Mariamov, whose teeth were chattering at the time of Lenia's elevation. Although only a peripheral character in the novel, he is interesting as another example of the ideological "backwardness" of the inhabitants of Liubimov. Despite being a Communist official, Mariamov still cannot shed his peasant mentality, and remnants of religious "prejudices". When questioned by the bosses of N about Tikhomirov's ideology and about his possible intention of reviving religion, Mariamov flatly denies it: "'He won't re-open churches,' Mariamov muttered, taking advantage of an oratorial pause. 'As regards [revival] of capitalism or freedom, that is as you please, but as regards the Christian religion, you need not worry, Lenia won't revive it.'" And when pressed further, he declares that "'Lenia Tikhomirov is a sorcerer! Antichrist! Devils assist him!' And raising his only arm, Mariamov made a fervent, wide sign of the cross..."[217] After his testimony, Mariamov is led to an isolation cell, while the leaders of N. engage in a "discussion" on the course to be taken — a brilliant satire on "collective leadership," which is hardly collective. Comrade O starts with his interpretation of Lenia's telegram proclaiming the independence of Liubimov: "What does 'to all' mean? If they address themselves to *all*, they must love and cherish *all* landowners and capitalists, *all* unliquidated princes and barons, and the inciters of the Cold War, including the Pope of Rome who is only waiting for an appropriate moment to feast on the blood of the toiling masses... Let's read further: 'The freedom of citizens is guaranteed by law.' How should one understand the term 'freedom'? Freedom for whom? Why and what kind of freedom is needed in a free country? This means, they want *freedom* to sell their motherland, to trade wholesale and retail in human beings as they did during the period of slavery, *freedom* to close schools and hospitals and to open churches according to the order of the Vatican, and to burn on the fires of the Inquisition representatives of science, as they already once did with Giordano Bruno ... It won't come off! We won't allow it! Do you hear, citizen Mariamov, we won't allow it! They want too much ..."[218] After having talked himself into his usual fury, during which comrade O would "bang the table with his fists, scream, stamp his feet without knowing why" (a clear allusion to Khrushchev's tempers) he gives colonel Almazov the order to liquidate the revolution in a statement which is virtually untranslatable in its vulgarity: "Enemy propaganda has infected your subordinates. You, Colonel, will have to sniff at that arse yourself ... You can borrow about twenty young chaps from the militia. We don't want any obvious 'menstruations' — everything to be nice and cultured. Let them wear hats and ties like in a restaurant. Just an outing for the lads, a day in the country. No farting out of revolvers, unless you have to. A couple of machine guns won't do any harm, though, take them along. Pick up Tikhomirov and the other rowdies and bring them in quietly. Reestablish the prison. Restore telegraphic communication with N. However, no repression. Don't be over-zealous. Discipline. Legality. You may touch women by the tits, but no further. No consequences of the personality cult. I give you 24 hours for the wohle disinfection, and wish you luck ..."[219] A satirical portrait from the other side of the political spectrum, which should be mentioned to show that Tertz's barb is not only directed against his own Soviet types, is that of the American journalist, Harry Jackson. Introducing himself to Lenia by his nickname of "Old Gangster," working for the "bourgeois paper 'Farting Intriguer Inmouth oh America' ('Perdit intrigan vrot okh Amerika' — a partial allusion to "Voice of America") he comes to get some information as to how soon "the rotten regime of capitalist magnates" will be reestablished in Liubimov. Lenia's enigmatic replies to his questions, such as "when the crawfish on the hill will start whistling" (another allusion to Khrushchev's

mannerisms and use of proverbs in his foreign interviews) make
him realize that he has met a match in him. Finally, Mr. Jackson
confesses that all he really wants is to buy Lenia's secret of transforming man's consciousness for any amount of money ("The
economic crisis is no joke, growing unemployment is pressing us,
one can't kill off everybody with the atom bomb") in order to turn
humanity *back* on the way of progress. The interview ends,
however, with Lenia transforming Mr. Jackson's consciousness:
". . . he left the appearance of Harry Jackson intact, but what did
he do to the bourgeois psychology of this inveterate tourist? He
did not leave a whole spot in it. He grabbed it by the gills, by the
core of his soul, and turned it so that it would renounce itself
according to all points, and would prove its inability to compete
with a Russian in the critique of pure reason . . ."[220] The heavy-
handedness of this satire speaks for itself.

Some critics have seen a broader political satire in the
"history" of Liubimov. Thus Boris Filippov considers it to be "the
history of the immense Communist world — primarily that of the
Communist USSR."[221] Andrew Field saw in it, similarly, "the
history of the Soviet Union from its beginning to the present day,"
with Lenia Tikhomirov being an "amalgam of Lenin and Stalin."[222]
The parallel to Saltykov-Shchedrin's history of the town of Glupov
— an extremely distorted, satirical representation of Russian
history — had been likewise cited. While Tertz's intentionally
ambiguous and "dense" storytelling is conducive to a wide variety
of interpretations, the question arises how far a given text can and
should be stretched. No doubt, Tertz was aware of Saltykov-
Shchedrin (he refers to him in his essay on Gor'kii), and certain
formal devices in his presentation, a few episodes, and possibly
even the name of the town — Liubimov, a contrast to Glupov —
seem to echo the former work.[223] However, on closer analysis it
becomes obvious that Tertz is not telling a satirical history of the

USSR, but is rather presenting a historical-philosophical satire. The "identity" of Lenia Tikhomirov, as Tertz conceived it, should provide an important clue to an interpretation of *Liubimov*. Even if Lenia's slit eyes may have been "borrowed" by Tertz from Lenin's image, there is little other evidence to connect him with Lenin or Stalin, for that matter.[224] Lenia is definitely not a concrete historical portrait; besides, he is building Communism *upon* Communism that already exists, making the idea of historical symbolism rather questionable. Even his status as a symbolical leader of a movement is intentionally lowered by Tertz. He hits on his idea by accident, somewhat like H. G. Wells's George Mc Whirter Fartheringay ("The Man Who Could Work Miracles"), a poor clerk in a department store, who suddenly discovers that he can perform miracles by an effort of his will.[225] Furthermore, Lenia is actually only a "shell," an instrument of his eccentric ancestor, Samson Samsonovich Proferansov, and as such, properly speaking, not even quite responsible for his action. "We are all thieves and prostitutes," the narrator in "The Icicle" had stated, speaking of the impossibility of isolating one's spiritual and physical ego from that of one's ancestors or successors. Lenia is a "talented executor" of the will of Samson Samsonovich, and only as long as the latter wishes him to be that. The will of Samson Samsonovich is that of the humanitarian, "atheistic, tolerant, purposeless" 19th century, which was seeking a religion, a Purpose, which would realize the paradise on earth man had always sought. It seems an ironic commentary on Communism, that it *cannot* be achieved in its ideal form without changing man's essence, his consciousness.

It seems that the Liubimov "experiment" is not so much illustrative of concrete history (the history of the Soviet Union), as of Tertz's general theory of history as a succession of various Purposes, whether it be Christianity, Democracy or Communism (cf. the essay on socialist realism). Each Purpose, upon which mankind seizes, is exclusive, rejects it predecessors, and goes through a period of rise, consolidation and decay, only to be followed by the next experiment in man's spiritual quest. Communism, A. D. 1958 is not what its ideals had promised, and thus Tertz catapults a whole historical epoch — the rise, bloom, and collapse of "ideal" Communism — into a short period of time, and into the spatially limited experiment at Liubimov.

Not only does Tertz show that each historical Purpose seems to be doomed to destruction, he also presents the eternal dilemma of ends and means, and of individual freedom. And in the final analysis Tertz echoes again Dostoevskii's questions in "Notes from Underground": the question whether material happiness in a regulated, Utopian society can outweigh the loss of individual freedom, whether an allegedly ideal Purpose can be justified by means of slavery over the mind and the body. Whether, finally, rationality and reason can and should prevail over irrationality and faith?

Lenia can bring on his reforms only by constantly "brainwashing" the citizens of Liubimov. "Don't steal, don't kill, don't forge documents, and don't commit any other crimes which lower the high dignity of man", Lenia suggests to the amnestied criminals when he opens the prison of Liubimov. "Remember, the word 'man' is a proud word."[226] He sends workers to build canals with hypnotic commands: "Keep your head high! Wider the step! Gayer the smile! Remember: nobody forces you to work! You yourself want to overfulfill the norm by 200 percent. Yes, yes, not less at all! You feel enthusiasm in your breast, you feel tirelessness in your muscles. You thirst to pierce your spades into the loam as soon as possible ..."[227]

Lenia influences the mind of a simple peasant woman who comes to him to get some straw, for he had not abolished "the ancient Russian custom of having people come with the least trivia to the Czar himself." He suggests that she should give up her small-scale farming, and devote herself to "the study of internal combustion" instead. In this extremely comical scene, the peasant woman, under Lenia's hypnotism, goes virtually overboard in her new interests: " 'It's so right, you hit exactly the mark, you expressed all my internal mechanics,' the widow sang, having grown younger by about 15 years, and getting confused at the multiplicity of perspectives that had opened up before her, 'take also my piglet, and the four chicken. To hell with them. I am worn out with them. They deprive me of my cultural development. Hey, I'll become a tractor driver, will put on pants, will take a seat behind the steering wheel! Where is my tractor?' "[228] Lenia has to restrain her ardor, by taking as a "voluntary contribution" only her piglet, Bor'ka by name.

Attempts at immoral behavior are also quelched by Lenia, and when a drunken peasant attempts to rape a girl in a distant vegetable plot, he immediately sends a hypnotic wave toward him. Letting the girl's "weak body out of his paws" the would-be criminal makes a polite apology: "Forgive me, madam, my bad behavior. It will never be repeated, I swear it to you by my honor!"[229]

The philosophical rather than political aspect of *Liubimov* is also reinforced by the presence of some obvious Christian symbolism. In his essay on socialist realism Tertz had pointed out some similarities between the Christian faith and the Communist "religion." To point to this once more, Tertz presents such scenes as Lenia's wedding to Serafima Petrovna, with Lenia changing water into wine and performing other miracles (an obvious allusion to the wedding feast at Cana). Serafima Petrovna's attempt to seduce her husband's disciple, Vitia Kochetov, is suggestive of the temptation of Joseph by Potiphar's wife. The man who dies of overdrinking is found lying with his palms extended "like Jesus

Christ," and here Lenia's powers are of no avail — he cannot resurrect the dead, for the mystical and otherworldly regions are closed to him.

Lenia's reign is of this world, materialistic, technologically oriented. During his short rule over Liubimov, he tries not only to establish the "proper" order in the town, but his plans (like those of many dictators) go further. He thinks about achieving such concentration of will power as to "move all humanity from its dead point, and then gradually to start the subjugation of the Antarctic and the industrial development of other planets." He imagines how "the governments of the greatest nations would put down their arms, open their frontiers, and the grateful people, of their free will, without coercion, would fall into his arms."[230] He even torments himself about the new name which he would give to Liubimov, after having it declared the capital of the globe, vascillating in his choice between "Sun-City" and "Tikhomirgorod" (Tikhomirov-City).[231]

The problem which Lenia and other "Weltbeglücker" like him have not taken into account, is the fact that man does not want regulated happiness, if he has no freedom. In a rather funny vision Savelii Kuzmich (who shares many of Lenia's views) imagines the blessings of an Utopian, push-button happiness, where everything is provided — from food to sex: "You push a button, and here, in a private room where you sit and jump up and down on a soft divan without leaving your place, a table appears before you like a phantom, covered with food and bottles of wine. (Hard liquors, I assume, will even then be rationed with the assistance of the government) [The Narrator's note]. You eat your way through it, you eat so much that you are ready to burst, and then you realize that the only thing which is missing in your life are cocoanuts which are not on the table, and you feel so insulted and lonely because of this neglect of your requirements that you feel like going and hanging yourself ... You push a button, and there without human interference, a self-moving small wagon on wheels appears before you, filled to the brim with all sorts of cocoanut fruit. But you have already stopped wanting them, and you say grimacing: 'Take away this rotten stuff, I don't need your favors!' And again you push the button in order to change the cocoanuts for something more interesting.

In response to your call, from a hole in the floor hidden in the parquet, jumps out on springs a blond maiden of marvellous beauty. You push the button and everything is o.k. You push it a second time, and again everything is fine. You push the same button a third time..." And yet this vision (which includes a pushbutton trip around the world and to the planets) ends in an unexpected rejection of such regulated "happiness," and desire for the primitive, irrational: "... And you will say, grimacing: 'So what, did you get your fill (doprygalis')? Have you reached all heights? You started with the locomotive and how did it end? It would be better for me to rot away with lice, it would be better for me to hang in my primeval state head down, swinging by the tail from the eucalyptus branch...' And man will start drinking from grief, as a sign of protest. He will start stealing hard liquor, vodka, marafet, regulated by the government. He will become a hooligan. He will start unscrewing screws, cutting wires with a knife, smashing lampignons in the sky with a catapult ..."[232]

A similar thought crosses even Lenia's one-track mind when at the height of the wedding celebration he is confronted with the corpse of the thief who died of overindulgence in his "alcohol": "Well, you strange man," Lenia addresses the corpse in his thoughts, "is it freedom that you wanted? What other freedom, if you got more than enough?" And he adds: "Yes, perhaps you are right. I have failed to take something into account."[233]

As already mentioned, drinking in Tertz's view is an act of defiance, a triumph of irrationality over rationality, the victory of the soul over the body (cf. "At the Circus," "Thoughts at Random"). At the beginning of the wedding celebration the narrator speaks of the Russians' need for drink: ". . . And we use drink for the strengthening of life and for warming up the soul, we only then begin to live when we drink, and we soar with our soul up, and rise over the immovable matter . . ."[234] Lenia who like Dostoevskii's Grand Inquisitor had attempted to liberate man of all his weaknesses and to provide for all his needs, finds himself finally rejected: "For their sake he had sacrificed his life, had undermined his health, but as soon as his energy gave way, the coarse savages were quick to jeer at their powerless commander. With their consent and for their benefit they had been taught discipline, were freed of their shortcomings, hardened in labor, took part in requisitionings . . ."[235]

The need for the spiritual, miraculous rather than the material, rational cannot be eradicated in man. This is clearly shown in the reactions of the population of Liubimov who considers Lenia a magician or even Antichrist, or in the belief of the militia from the city of N. that he is a woodspirit (leshii). Getting lost just before reaching Liubimov, one of the men says: "It's the woodspirit who is leading us astray . . . Lesha, Lenia — the chief leading magician of these boggy parts . . ."[236] More than that, the narrator — whoever he may be at the time — suggests time and again the presence of the miraculous and supernatural. It comes out, very casually, in Savelii Kuzmich's narrative about the fate of all who took an active part in the demolition of an old miracle-working monastery: ". . . Around Christmas the chairman burned to death, Egor Tikhonovich Mariamov's [right] arm dried up, while two other exploders were killed at the time of the demolition by a dynamite wave, and a year later Andriusha Pashechnik who had

been the instigator to this, was hit by a tree trunk on his head ...
and he died toward morning ..."[237] In chapter 3, which describes
the strange experiences of colonel Almazov, the narrator in an
aside stresses the fact that there can be no rational explanation for
the manifestation of the irrational: "... there has been no man yet
who could have guessed and found out how the Evil One operates.
Why he howls in the chimney on winter evenings, why he scratches
under the floor, and moans in the moor with a hoarse, inhuman
voice ..."[238] As to the women who seem to be even less rational
than men, and whose need for faith is stronger, to them Lenia is
clearly a messenger of God. Watching the departure of the militia
to fight Liubimov, the women of N. mumble their blessings: "In
Liubimov a miracle-working icon has appeared ... Bishop
Leonid ... He is not a bishop, but a blessed, a fool-in-Christ, Lenia.
He is opening the churches! He is opening the churches! He is
opening the churches! O Lord, help him! Give him, o Lord, victory
over the hosts of Satan, over the hosts of Antichrist!"[239]

But the most obvious symbol of the primitive, irrational,
religious (and simultaneously, another example of the intransigence
of the mass to modern, Communist ideology) in the novel, is the
figure of Lenia's mother. She does not understand what her son is
doing, she does not care about it, her only concern is his physical
welfare, and her plea for him to have "some cottage cheese with
sour cream" runs like a leitmotif through the novel. At one point
Lenia tries to brainwash his mother, to free her too of religious
"prejudices" — at which point the narrator interferes and warns
Lenia — but the result is only an incoherent, grotesque babbling on
her part, which she immediately forgets: "There is no God. The
prophet Eliah has been shot. Electricity. Thunder comes out of
electricity, Leniushka, eat some cottage cheese with sour cream.
You are so thin, transparent ... There is no God ..."[240] And at the
end of the novel, Lenia's mother, ignorant of her son's fate, is seen

in a distant little church, praying for his safety, and listening to the solemn prayer for the dead of a simple village priest. And this lengthy prayer, with its solemn Church Slavonic diction, sounds like a final chord in stressing the religious element in the novel:

"'Our Father,' he cried out with stern solemnity: 'We grieve about the violence of the lawless blasphemers of Thy Name and Holiness ... Our Father, be merciful to those stricken with pernicious unbelief. Our Father, their sins are great but Thy mercy is greater. Our Father, forgive all those who have died unrepenting. Our Father, save those who have ruined themselves in the dullness of their minds. Our Father, purify them for the sake of the faithful ones who cry out to Thee day and night. Our Father, forgive the parents for the sake of their innocent babies. Our Father, let the tears of mothers expiate the sins of the children ...'"[241] Behind the scepticism, irony and mockery of the novel seems to lie a fervent desire for faith.

As already mentioned, the motif of physical re-incarnation plays an important role in the novel. The "father" of the "scientific revolution" in Liubimov, Samson Samsonovich Proferansov, becomes reincarnated in the 20th century in the figure of an elderly professor who suggests to Savelii Kuzmich (then a young man) to write a Chronicle of Liubimov, and then transfers part of his powers to Lenia, and part to Savelii Kuzmich who writes with his help. It is because of this general fluidity of personalities and perhaps also because of the weight of philosophical ideas in the novel, which makes the characters in *Liubimov* difficult to define. Lenia, as has been pointed out, is less an original character than a symbol of a dictator, and a "shell" designed to execute for a certain time, the will of Samson Samsonovich. He is too simple-minded and limited to be the hero of a novel, and all his revolutionary ideas come to him from the "beyond." If there *is* a hero in the novel, it is the city of Liubimov which for a short time has the potential of the realization of a dream: "Get up, you have slept enough!" the narrator (who this time is not Savelii Kuzmich) says (chapter 3). "The day of your glory has come! Here is power for you which is sufficient to make all your dreams a reality. Here, satisfy your longing for a benevolent and mighty Czar. I give you a leader endowed with unnoticeable power, about whom you have been dreaming for three hundred years . . ."[242] However, Liubimov, for better or for worse, proves to be unable to live up to expectation, and the dream ends in anarchy and destruction.

More complex and interesting than Lenia is the chronicler of Liubimov, Savelii Kuzmich, who beyond being the mouthpiece of Samson Samsonovich and Tertz himself, has also some individual features. Savelii Kuzmich is presented at first as a rather typical Soviet semi-intellectual (polu-intelligent) from the provinces, who spouts the official Soviet jargon, is somewhat simple-minded, politically adaptable and cowardly. The preface, in which Savelii Kuzmich describes the city of Liubimov (an example of the Zoshchenko-type *skaz* which Tertz had used before) gives a good idea of his mental horizon: ". . . But in itself the city of Liubimov is not bad, gay, and its inhabitants are culturally quite developed, interested, there are many Komsomol members, and a rather dense layer (prosloika) of intelligentsia . . . By the way, there are also some monuments of architecture. A former monastery from the middle-ages. After the revolution, in 1926, when the holy fathers were exiled to the Solovki to occupy themselves with corrective labor, a professor [the re-incarnation of Samson Samsonovich] came to us for scientific explorations [to see] how it all had been in reality . . ."[243] Savelii Kuzmich's own youth, which explains his subsequent faible for Serafima Petrovna is described by him as follows: " Just girls were in [my] mind, bare buttocks and all sorts of flirtations, a self-teaching method for playing the guitar in 25 lessons. A bicycle . . ."[244]

It is relatively easy for Lenia to brainwash Savelii Kuzmich, who is happy to become the "official historiographer" of the new ruler. But as soon as Lenia's magnetic powers begin to wane, Savelii Kuzmich's loyalty begins to waver; he deserts him, and tries to ingratiate himself with the exiled former Party Secretary, Tishchenko: "How about it?" he asks the ex-Secretary whom he finds at the outskirts of the city fishing: "I think I am the first . . . Take it into consideration, Semen Gavrilovich, the very first in the city . . . who arrived to assure you of my faithfulness to the general line, and to say that we will not tolerate . . ."[245] It turns out, unfortunately, that he had not been the first.

Very soon after he starts the Liubimov Chronicle, the presence of Samson Samsonovich asserts itself in Savelii Kuzmich's writing. For while at first he has great difficulties in putting his thoughts on paper, soon he gets the feeling that he is "put in motion by somebody's invisible hand" (cf. the same motif in "The Graphomaniacs"). This is followed by a conversation between Savelii Kuzmich and an invisible Samson Samsonovich (like Mariamov, Savelii Kuzmich also harbors in his soul religious "prejudices," and takes the voice, at first, for a manifestation of the devil) in which the latter tells him that they are writing in "layers": ". . . I will help you and will gladly take on myself parts of the descriptions. That is, you will, of course, do the writing, but the thoughts will come from a completely different source . . . We are all endowed with powers by someone who is older than we are . . ."[246] When Savelii Kuzmich tries to rebel and insists on writing without Samson Samsonovich's help, the result is pure gibberish. The further cooperation between Savelii Kuzmich and Samson Samsonovich encounters no difficulties.

The voice of Tertz himself is also heard through Savelii Kuzmich at times, as e.g. when he expounds the official Soviet demand for realist literature: "Only one thing is bitter — that is when the writer suddenly goes off into fantasy. You are sitting here, feeling deeply, and perhaps chills are running up and down your spine, and he, it turns out, invented it all out of the blue. No, if you start to write, then you must write about things which you saw yourself, or at least, which you heard from trustworthy sources. So that the reader's soul, travelling over the pages, would not spoil its precious eyesight in vain, but would receive reliable and useful information for its spiritual development . . ."[247]

The motif of fear and persecution — so strong in Tertz's stories — is also voiced by Savelii Kuzmich. At the beginning of his Chronicle he is already prepared to renounce it: "If stern judges will call me to answer, if they put my hands and feet into iron, I warn you ahead of time: I will renounce everything, as sure as death, I will renounce it! Hey! I will say, citizens judges! You have confused me, you have got me involved in something. Shoot, if you wish, but I am not guilty!"[248] At the end (a year after the Revolution has been eradicated) Savelii Kuzmich fearfully begs Samson Samsonovich for help: ". . . Our situation could not be worse. Trials are going on. Soon arrests will start again in the city. I sit here and am fearful that they will search me and find this manuscript under the floor planks, and then through it they will get hold of all of us. Listen, Professor. You are my co-author. Hide for the time being, somewhere, our tale. Let it lie for a while in some inaccessible safe. You took the manuscript from Lenia. You must have a hiding place. Some secret little place. Give it shelter until an appropriate time. Isn't it your property?"[249] And here again, Savelii Kuzmich seems to assume some features of his author, and to echo Tertz's own feelings and fears.

Another "shell" is Serafima Petrovna Kozlova, the short-lived "Czarina" of Liubimov. Like Lenia, she is less a character in her own right than a symbol; this time, of "black magic," the feminine sex, and ultimately of the irrational, chaos and anarchy.

Incidentally, this seems to be the case with most of Tertz's feminine characters, with the only exception of Natasha in "The Icicle." Savelii Kuzmich's first description of her as an example of the intellectual élite of Liubimov is both comical and telling: "In all amateur theatricals, picnics, she would play the lead. At namesday's parties she would gulp down a glass of champagne, yell, turn pale, and immediately go off dancing the lezginka with a knife blade between her teeth — all you could see would be her elbows flying..."[250] Her transformation from a *femme fatale* to Lenia's slave is due to his magnetic powers. Lenia regulates her behavior by giving her various doses of his brainwaves: making her docile and loving, completely submissive, crawling before him on the floor, or letting her regain some of her former haughtiness. However, Serafima Petrovna's love for Lenia remains unrequited: Lenia does not love her in her submissive condition; besides, he cannot expand his psychic energies on sex, and thus the royal marriage remains forever unconsummated. And as Lenia's powers begin to wane, Serafima Petrovna returns to her former dissolute self. One of her last acts in the novel is an attempt to seduce her husband's only faithful follower, Vitia Kochetov, by inciting him to flee with her, and opening before him vistas of political power and glory:

"... In Leningrad we will construct the perpetuum mobile ourselves, according to the plans. [One of Lenia's pet projects prior to his take-over of Liubimov had been the construction of a perpetuum mobile.] We'll raise a new banner. We'll lead an army against Liubimov ... I'll bear you a son. You will become my prince consort. Vice roy. Favorite. I assure you, Mao Tse Tung will offer us his hand in friendship. In the worst case we'll sacrifice Central Asia for a time. We'll give up the Caucasus. We'll spread the conflagration to Europe. Don't play jokes with me, Vitia! I don't have some [puny] regional center in mind. I promise you . . ."[251] By a tremendous effort of willpower, Vitia refuses Serafima Petrovna's offers. And even before Liubimov is overrun by amphibious tanks, she flees to disappear from the city for ever.

The form of the novel — a parody on a historical Chronicle endowed with copious footnotes, describing important events as recorded by a humble chronicler — is as already mentioned clearly derived from Saltykov-Shchedrin's *History of a Town,* and ultimately perhaps from Pushkin's "History of the Village of Goriukhino." There are definite parallels in the presentation of one of the chroniclers of Glupov as a "fragile vessel" (skudel'nyi sosud) of glorification, and Savelii Kuzmich being an actual "vessel" of Samson Samsonovich's will, in the search of the respective chroniclers for material, in the description of humble provincial cities (Glupov's fame resting on its three rivers, seven hills, and production of *kvas;* Liubimov being known for its moors and woods, inhabited by inedible birds), in what seems to be references to the *Igor Tale* in both novels, etc. Certain episodes, already pointed out, such as the attempts of a mayor of Glupov, Ugrium-Burcheev (caricature of Arakcheev) to bring "order" to Glupov, to re-name it Nepreklonsk, and to make it an ideal of human existence by forcing everyone to work on commando; the ill-fated expedition of mayor Borodavkin (caricature of Nicholas I) against the village Negodnitsa — all these episodes seem to have some reflection in Tertz. Tertz's irony is, of course, much less cruel than Saltykov-Shchedrin's, he does not describe actual personages, his storytelling is more complex, and more fantastic.

The flower of phantasmagoria and the grotesque blooms abundantly in *Liubimov,* and it is impossible to point out all its manifestations, except for the most striking ones. The whole biography of Samson Samsonovich, told to Lenia by Savelii Kuzmich, is a brilliant exercise in Gogolian nonsense, grotesque imagery and literary allusions. Samson Samsonovich, who according to

Savelii Kuzmich was a "philanthropist, theosophist, Diogenes and
partly a bibliomaniac" searching for the stone of wisdom or the
meaning of life, is presented as a contemporary of Lavoisier,
Tolstoi, Turgenev, Goncharov, Czar Nicholas I, as well as of the
1917 Revolution! There are nonsensical allusions to Pushkin,
Gogol', Esenin, as e.g. in the fact that Samson Samsonovich's nurse
was called Arina Rodionovna (like Pushkin's), that he proposed
to the governor's daughter (like Gogol''s Chichikov), that after a
trip to India on the frigate "Vitiaz' " (perhaps an allusion to Goncharov's travel on the "Frigate Pallada"), he greeted Arina
Rodionovna with lines from Esenin, etc. After his death he remains
a benevolent ghost in his old house, warning his posterity (although
he never seems to have married) of dangers and revolution.

An especially grotesque scene in which Samson Samsonovich's
ghost manifests itself in the post-revolutionary period is in a tea-
house, where an elderly Chekist suddenly heard an invisible voice
asking him: "Hello, call up Lavoisier, ask Trotskii — who will
restore to the heart love that has been lost? Who will encompass
with his eye the phantasies of creation?" When the Chekist looks
around he sees "an old man with an intellectual face . . . drinking
tea and reading a newspaper." The man then disappears in thin
air, and at the spot where he had been sitting, the Chekist and his
friend find an old 5 kopeck-piece (with the double-headed eagle),
a damp issue of "Izvestiia," and on the ceiling "damp traces of
feltboots disappearing in the direction of the clattering ventila-
tor. . ."[252] And in an apparently strange, but meaning-laden switch
of subject, Savelii Kuzmich justifies the escapades of Samson Sam-
vich by the example of Lenin, who allegedly while "recuperat-
ing and composing at nights the first Five Year Plan, would run
out into the yard of his dacha and bay at the moon . . ." And "if
even Lenin, Vladimir Il'ich, — I want to stress this, — had his
moods, then why should not a good Russian gentleman have

them, who did not even do any harm to anyone, and who got into the ultimate heights in a more sure way . . ."[253]

Another grotesque scene is colonel Almazov's encounter with a strange creature which hypnotizes him and turns him and his "army" away from Liubimov (chapter 3): ". . . [he] noticed on the branch a big-headed bird of a dirty-green color which resembled a big, overfed toad. 'What a bird. That's not a bird, but a real crocodile,' he said, without any hunter's enthusiasm, however . . ."[254] And instead of trying to find the lost road to Liubimov, the colonel, under the hypnotic stare of the beast reviews his life, thinks about the women who had loved him, and who "taking over his gallant manners" had called him "mon amour" or "mon colonel." And finally, at the moment when he is about to fall asleep, he hears the strange bird-crocodile speak to him in pure Parisian accents: "Bonne nuit, mon amour. Vous m'avez fait un grand plaisir, mon brave colonel."[255]

Finally, at the end of the novel when Lenia's powers revive for the last time, his random, subconscious thoughts become immediately translated into action by the population of Liubimov: "Some, primarily women, bared themselves beyond the measure of decency. Others, primarily men, gathering in small groups, began to fight, which resembled friendly collective work: without shouting, without superfluous moans. Still others, primarily silly little children became like domestic animals, who also . . . not falling behind man took part in the meeting and in this alliance of the supreme power and popular freedom. Chicken crowed like roosters, goats tried to bark. A cow, miaowing, jumped over a fance. A giant [young man] feeling like a bull, took heart, and turned toward his girl-friend . . ."[256] The widow who only recently had been eager to study internal combustion under Lenia's influence, rides through the air on a broom ("A real witch," Lenia thought of her, and this thought was immediately translated into reality), and disappears talking gibberish. And just as suddenly as it began, the madhouse scene ends as Samson Samsonovich withdraws his magnetic powers from Lenia. When the latter calls out to a chicken, even that creature does not obey him, and continues to "occupy itself with its trashy trade . . ."

The style of *Liubimov*, beyond its connection to pseudo-Chronicles, is a perfect example of Tertz's ornamental, many-layered, heterogeneous way of writing. The disruption of time sequence (chapter 1 follows in time the events of chapter 2), and the splitting up of the narrative voice into at least two (and some-times even three) voices, presents grave problems in delineation. Although in the preface, Savelii Kuzmich presents himself as the main chronicler of the events in Liubimov ("be our Leo Tolstoi, our mirror of the Revolution," Lenia tells him subsequently), very soon the voice of Samson Samsonovich asserts itself (chapter 3), corrects and directs Savelii Kuzmich, and even takes over some chapters. Even more, a third voice, an anonymous "I" makes itself heard with some philosophical asides and literary metaphors, reflecting once more the author himself.

The preface, with its folksy, Zoshchenko-type style is clearly attributable to Savelii Kuzmich. The next 2 chapters which describe the events of May 1 (chapter 1) and the events leading up to them (chapter 2), also seem to belong to him. But then the anonymous narrator (the "I") takes over part of chapter 3, which is then apparently continued by Samson Samsonovich until chapter 5. The biography of Samson Samsonovich, told by Savelii Kuzmich is, as mentioned before, an accumulation of grotesque nonsense. Chapters 6 and 7 are presented partly by an unidentifiable narrator (Samson Samsonovich or the "I"), partly by Savelii Kuzmich, who concludes the novel. Not only make these constant switches for a conglomeration of various stylistic features, even the identifiable voices show no unity in their manner of writing. Savelii Kuzmich's

relatively low intellectual level does not prevent him from recording the fight for power between Party secretary Tishchenko and
Lenia in terms of a parody on transformations common in folk-
tales: [Tishchenko] "... fell from the tribune, hit his head against
the ground, and disappeared, and from the hole which appeared
at the place where he fell, rose with loud crowing a black raven,
all decked out in plumes! ... Then Leonid Ivanovich, being no fool,
ran and hit the same spot with his open chest, and immediately his
hands showed the structure of wings, his legs grew shorter and hid
under his stomach, and his new steel-gray suit, almost without
changing color was used for his external feathers. Lenia's beak grew
crooked, became bony, his eyes became round, blinked, and here
you have a fighting hawk quite ready to battle the crowing Semen
Gavrilovich ..."[257] At the moment when Lenia is about to
overcome his adversary, Tishchenko transforms himself into a fox,
while Lenia becomes a greyhound; then Tishchenko assumes the
guise of a riderless bicycle, while Lenia that of a motorcycle ...
Savelii Kuzmich stops the description by announcing suddenly that
this was not reality, but the creation of a popular myth, "not
supported by fact." Savelii Kuzmich's aside on the Jews whose sad
eyes reflect the desert from which they originally came, and who
remind the Russians of the eternity of history, his elaborate comparison of a bouquet of flowers with literature (chapter 6), also
hardly fit his original simple image. His final, philosophical remark
on the Russian character is also clearly attributable to Tertz: "In
Russia clever men have through the ages passed for fools, and
honest men for scoundrels. And this is for no other reason than
because of our Russian conscience which tells us that it is not
becoming for man to bare his bashful soul unless he has first
covered it with some filth. Sometimes you will swear and lie, and
even steal a little, and at times you may undertake an irresponsible
act with the wife of a neighbor in a hayloft, and all this with one

aim — to preserve the soul intact, under a cuirass, which like a jewel in a casket, needs a safe lock . . ."[258]

The authorical remarks (which can be separated even less from those of Samson Samsonovich than those of Savelii Kuzmich) are similarly heterogenous in style, starting with the elaborate and grotesque aside on dreams (chapter 3), and ending with a folksy aside on trouser pockets — the only asylum for a lonely man (chapter 7). The description of the sleepy town of Liubimov — asleep both literally and figuratively — is reminiscent of a similar vision by the narrator in the prologue to "The Trial Begins:" "With outstretched bare feet, lying on their backs or bellies, people are motionless like corpses. But it is only in appearance that they are so peaceful, for what is going on there, inside, under the cover of brows, where they have retired to early last night, in crowds, holding their breath? . . . There a feast is going on, people are running, pushing, passions are boiling, glasses are clinking, and some anemic poor chap astride the governor's daughter carries out a world revolution for the nth time . . . Hurry, hurry to have your fill of sleep! You don't have much time," the narrator calls to them, for Liubimov is destined to realize its dreams of a "benevolent and mighty Czar . . ."[259] But at the end of the novel when the dream fails, the author understands that the course of history cannot be known to man (in obvious contrast to Marx's claim): "Who will tell: where is the source of the fall of great dynasties? When did the decline of Europe, the fall of Rome begin? Perhaps, at its zenith, at the hour of its greatest glory, some far-seeing genius was already departing from the dull shores. Perhaps, some historical power only just appeared in the world and had no time to develop its industry and to erect on earth its architectural monument, and in the mysterious book there is already written the conclusion that in the course of so and so many hours it will be wiped off the face of the earth by some other historical power, which, in its turn, will end in the same confusion . . ."[260] It is this remark which seems to provide the most real clue to an understanding of the "history" of Liubimov.

In another aside, the author warns the reader (or himself?) of dispersed thoughts (rasseiannye mysli) which lead to no good. Literary comparisons and metaphors which show that this "I" is often the spokesman for the author, occur in various parts of the novel, as e.g. at the beginning of chapter 6, where a comparison is made between a carrier pigeon flying home and an author finishing his novel: "His native pigeon cote attracted him — like the finale of an unfinished novel, rising before the eye of its Author, pulls out the slippery thread of a plot into a line. Let the heroes storm and run around on the stage of life in fruitless endeavors to lengthen the burden of existence. The dénouement is already known to the inspired Master, and he rubs his hands, looking forward to the end of the work, and rushes toward the goal like a pigeon let out of his basket."[261] Another striking image, suggestive of Maiakovskii, is the metaphorical presentation of Lenia's struggle with enemy airplanes, which seems to become a symbolical presentation of the writer vis à vis the totalitarian state: ". . . His [Lenia's] face, stretched out on the cobble-stones, the whole length of the market square, was an excellent target, and the pilot knew that to kill a man who is lying on his back is just as simple as to plow up with a fire bomb a forest wilderness. That's it, he knew and saw that the haggard cheeks of Leonid Ivanovich are subject to burning no less than the banks of ravines covered with dry spurge (molokhai). That his lips, covered with hillocks of bog rash are powerless to resist the blow. That his eyes . . . Wait! What comparison should we quickly find for human eyes that have no other weapon than his despair fixed on high . . . You may say perhaps, who cares about comparisons, and why carry on this nonsense, when the whole situation is clear, and is it worthy to cover the vanquished hero with a clumsy, oldfashioned metaphor? . . . We do not agree !! If we had only one battery, only some poor carbine, we would not shatter the sky with coarse outcries. But where is justice?! They have airplanes, newspapers, journals, radio, insane asylums, telephone, and we — nothing, well you understand, nothing in our hands. [Only] our bared imagination. So won't we, pressed down to the earth and waiting for the hour of death, rush forward and poke into the purring nozzle the first monstrous, bleeding hyperbole that comes to mind?!"[262] It is fairly obvious that in this instance Tertz is speaking of literature as the only weapon in the struggle with tyranny.

These few examples of the various devices used by Tertz do not, by far, exhaust the topic. There are many other features that could be mentioned, as e.g. his favorite "surrealist" device of disjointed words (e.g. Vitia's thoughts at the moment of temptation by Serafima Petrovna in chapter 6). However, they hardly add much to the overall interpretation of the novel.

Liubimov is a difficult book, a book of ideas in a Dostoevskian sense, covered up by buffoonery and fantasy, and Tertz himself seems to like to assume the guise of a fool-in-Christ (iurodivyi) in his work, in order to cover up, and to keep intact the most important aspect of himself, his soul.

5. "Thoughts at Random" ("Mysli vrasplokh")[263]

This collection of seemingly unconnected random thoughts, aphorisms, philosophical reflections and short episodes, is the most personal among Tertz's works. It provides some new and interesting insight into the writer's complex and paradoxical personality, and reinforces and repeats some ideas from his fiction. As to whether such literary "confessions" can be accepted as accurate reflections of the author himself is open to debate. There is some inevitable stylization, literary embellishment and distortion, and conscious or unconscious "borrowing." In the case of Tertz the example of Vasilii Rozanov,[264] both in tone and general subject matter, comes to mind. Rozanov, "the great heresy of Russian literature"[265] whose spiritual geneology seems to issue from the Russian fools-in-Christ (iurodivye) was one of the most striking literary personalities of the early 20th century. Rozanov's total "baring" of his self, his preoccupation with his soul, God, death, Russia are themes that are close to Tertz. There is even a certain parallelism to Rozanov in the formulation of some of Tertz's thoughts and aphorisms.[266] It is only in the theme of sex which Rozanov elevated to the status of an Old Testament myth, where Tertz differs from him completely. For here Tertz shows a strong rejection of the flesh and an asceticism which in its severity is reminiscent of the late Tolstoi.

In Tertz's overall work, the "Thoughts" are important in at least two ways: first, in their emotional, highly personal aspect they complement the rational philosophical and literary theories in "What is Socialist Realism?" Second, they seem to point to a certain development in Tertz in the direction of a deeper, spiritual conception of life.

As the title indicates, the "Thoughts" do not attempt to present any unified body of thought, but rather alternate between impersonal sketches, and personal thoughts and comments. Among the former an alleged dialogue between two women could be cited: "Do you have a husband?" one asks the other. "For the night — yes, but otherwise — no," the latter answers.[267] Or a parable-like story could be mentioned in which an old peasant woman forbids her son to cut off her long toenails for she will need them to climb up the hill to reach God when she dies. These sketches are reminiscent of Tolstoi's late parables and Rozanov's short stories.

However, they occupy a relatively minor part in Tertz's "Thoughts." For the largest part of the "Thoughts" is concerned with Tertz's personal ideas, feelings and impressions. And here one finds that certain themes are repeated, with some variations, time and again. Interestingly, the theme of art is virtually absent from the "Thoughts." What Tertz is concerned with, are rather, the ultimate "essentials" of being — body, soul, God, death.

Tertz's love for paradox is nowhere as clearly expressed as in his attitude toward the human body. On one hand, it is necessary as the only cover which the soul has: "... To make a screen of the body, a walking barricade, and to hide behind it. If there were just the soul — could we stand it? How can the soul turn away, how can it cover itself up? The soul cannot even close its eyelids. It is always visible..."[268] On the other hand Tertz feels a disgust for the body which seems to him an inferior part of his being. Like the hero of his story, "Pkhents," he is repulsed by the physical manifestations of the body: "For some reason dirt and garbage are concentrated around man. In nature, you do not find this. Animals do not produce dirt if they are not in a shed, or a cage, i.e. again under the power of man... Man, on the other hand, from morning till night has to clean up after himself. Sometimes this process gets so boring that one thinks: if only one could die quickly in order not to create dirt and not to dirty oneself."[269] Tertz is repulsed by gluttony, another aspect of man's physical being, and, of course, by sex. Tertz's negative feelings evoked by sex move on two levels — the aesthetic and the moral, with the latter definitely predominating. "The location of the sexual organs — in the immediate vicinity of the organs of secretion — is murderous. As if nature itself envisaged a grimace, full of sarcasm, disgust. That which is located next to urine and faeces cannot be pure, spiritual. A physically unpleasant, stinking surrounding cries out about the stigma on our genitals (sramnye chasti) . . ."[270] Tertz seems to be torn in a struggle between the attraction of the flesh ("I was the 67th for her, she was the 44th for me,") and attempts at its mortification: "If only one could become an eunuch, how much one could achieve!"[271] he exclaims. In this struggle with sexual desire and the feeling of the sinfulness of the flesh Tertz is reminiscent of the late Tolstoi. Yet although Tertz finds something "pathological" in man's sexual relations, he cannot refrain from occasional cynical remarks, such as "In relations with women it is always more important to take off her panties than to satisfy one's natural inclinations. And the higher and less accessible that woman is, the most interesting it is. . ."[272] Women, except as symbols of "black magic-sex," have no place in Tertz's "Thoughts," and this explains perhaps the absence of convincing, three-dimensional, sympathetic feminine characters in his fiction. They are typed either as *femme fatales* (Marina in "The Trial Begins," Serafima Petrovna in *Liubimov*), or as passive, peripheral figures (Natasha in "The Icicle," Lida in "You and I," Zinaida in "The Graphomaniacs," Veronika in "Pkhents"). And yet, in the final analysis, after all his violent indictment of sex, Tertz finds partial justification for it in practice, in life. For it may be not only a sinful search for pleasure, but also "a striving for the far 'beyond,' pity for oneself, and a desire to occupy oneself somehow, to go away, to change the environment, and even love of one's neighbor whom we cannot caress in any other way . . ."[273]

Still, the primacy of the soul over the body is unquestionable for Tertz: "Perhaps life consists in the cultivation of the soul, yes, yes that very same, immortal soul which will replace you and will fly away . . ."[274] The theory of physical reincarnation (in lieu of immortality of the soul) which was so prominent in Tertz's fiction ("The Icicle," *Liubimov*) has no place in Tertz's "Thoughts". For it is the soul which is the only eternal, imperishable, valuable component of man. "One should keep in close contact with one's soul," says Tertz, so that it "would remember you, would become friends with you, and because of this would preserve a part of your personality."[275] And in interpreting the Russian expression for "ruining one's soul" (pogubit' dushu), he comes to the conclusion that the *soul* cannot be ruined, only *man* can be ruined by losing his soul. For "the soul does not depend on you, but you depend on it, and are under its tutelage, if you have time to notice it."[276]

This ascetic, spiritual trend in Tertz's "Thoughts" inevitably leads to God and to religious questions. And here it becomes clear for the first time that Tertz has a deep (if not quite conventional) religious attitude. Already in his essay on socialist realism Tertz spoke about the impossibility of freedom of choice in matters of faith (whether it be Communism, which he classified as a kind of "religion," or conventional religion) — either you believe or you don't. In "Thoughts" this idea is repeated again: "Freedom is always negative and presupposes lack, emptiness, which longs for the quickest possible fulfilment . . ."[277] Tertz must have found that Marxism or Communism could not fulfil his spiritual needs, and so he turned to God, with a deep longing for faith: "O Lord, manifest Yourself before me," he says. "Confirm that You hear me. I don't ask for a miracle — only for some barely noticeable sign. Well, for instance, that a bug would fly out of a bush . . . Nobody would suspect anything. But for me it would be enough. I would immediately guess that You hear me and make me understand this . . ."[278] Although Tertz can conceive of God in terms of an abstract idea (". . . He embraces everything and is all-present, as the most important [essence] which cannot be confined to anything. It is the greatest, only manifestation in life. Besides it there is nothing."),[279] his preference seems to be for a simple faith in the reality of God: ". . . Such conviction [in the reality of the kingdom of God] is often lacking in our philosophic-theological structures. Everything is conceived so spiritually that it becomes unclear whether God really exists, or whether he is only a symbol of our humane inclinations. A savage who imagines God in the shape of a blood-thirsty animal blasphemes less than a philosopher idealist who has substituted Him by a gnoseological allegory."[280] Tertz would like to trust in God "like a dog trusts his master. You whistle — it comes. And no matter where you may go, it will run after you, without asking or thinking anything, happily even up to the end of the world."[281] And this idea is once more poignantly expressed in words suggestive of a profession of faith: "One must believe not because of tradition, not out of fear of death, not 'just in case,' not because somebody orders it, and something frightens you, not out of humanitarian principles, not in order to be saved, nor for the sake of originality. One must believe for the very simple reason that God exists."[282]

In his search for a real God Tertz turns to Christ ("who ... rose literally, tangibly, in the flesh, and appeared as a manifestation [ochevidnost'], despite the abstractions of Pharisees"),[283] and his ideals of asceticism and poverty which seem to have a strong appeal for Tertz. Modern man with his ego-centrism and desire for acquisition — "money, knowledge, books, fame, women, travel, even suffering," — is contrasted with the selflessness of Christ. Tertz goes even so far as to consider that "any personality is repulsive, if there is a lot of it. Personality is always a capital, even if it consisted of virtue, mind, and talent." "'Distribute all your goods' ... Christ loved those who were 'nobodies'. And wasn't he himself a 'nobody'?" For in him there was no "vampirism of genius" but the "selflessness of holiness which shines not by its own, but by Your light, O Lord!"[284] "Blessed are the poor in spirit" seems to be the leitmotif of Tertz's religious thought.

Although the Christian ideals are contrary to man's basic nature ("you are beaten, and yet you are happy ... You don't run away from death, but long for it"),[285] they can make man truly happy. For once he learns to substitute his essence for another (Christian) essence, which "teaches to be ill, to suffer, to die, and which delivers one of the duty of fear and hatred,"[286] he will be truly freed. Christianity, according to Tertz, "carries out the role of the shock regiment . . . thrown into the most dangerous and heated segment of the battle line."[287] It is "the religion of greatest hope, born out of desperation, the religion of chastity, established on the sharpest realization of its sinfulness, the religion of the resurrection of the flesh in the midst of stench and putrefaction."[288]

In going back to the source of early Christianity — Christ — Tertz reveals himself also as a traditionalist in regard to the church. "The church cannot help but be conservative," if it wants "to preserve faithfulness to tradition" and "to bring the aroma and smell of eternity" to us. It must not say "one thing today, another thing tomorrow, depending on the interests of progress."[289] And even if it should become petrified like a mummy, he believes that it will hear the hour of resurrection and will rise from the dead. Modern Christianity, on the other hand, in Tertz's opinion, sins on the side of mediocrity, on being "too well brought up, fearing dirt, coarseness, directness," and preferring to it "the golden means." Tertz longs for a more active, passionate involvement, even if it be heresy, for "heresy is not as dangerous now, as drying up in the roots:" "O Lord, better if I make a mistake in Your name than I forget You. Better I will sin in Your name than forget You. Better I will ruin my soul than You will disappear from my sight . . ."[290]

Tertz's traditionalism in regard to the church is further connected with strong Slavophile tendencies, and an idealization of the Russian peasant as a man who was "much more widely and firmly connected with the universal — historical and cosmic — life." And while modern man may go around the world in a matter of days, he won't gain anything from it for his soul. The Russian peasant, on the other hand, with the simple, intuitive gesture of crossing

himself before a meal "would connect himself with earth and
heaven, with the past and present." And when he died, he did it
"in the depths of the universe, next to Abraham," while "we die
alone on our narrow, useless couches . . ."[291] And nearly as idealistic,
in a Slavophile sense is Tertz's famous remark on the Russian
character ("infamous" for its heretical nature in the eyes of the
Soviet prosecutor), which has a Dostoevskian, prophetic ring:

"Drunkenness is our basic national vice, and even more,
or *idée fixe*. It is not from poverty and grief that the Russian
people drink, but because of the eternal need for the miraculous
and extraordinary, they drink, if you wish, mystically, tyring to
take the soul out of its terrestrial equilibrium, and to return it to
its blessed, incorporeal state. Vodka is the white magic of the
Russian peasant (muzhik); he prefers it decidedly to, black magic
the feminine sex . . . In connection with a tendency to steal (a lack
of firm faith in concrete connections among objects) drunkenness
gives us a vagabondish freedom and puts us in the suspicious
position of riffraff . . . This gives us an undisputed advantage in
comparison with the West, and at the same time puts upon the
life and the strivings of the nation a stamp of instability, frivolous
irresponsibility. We are capable of stealing Europe, or of letting into
it an interesting heresy, but we are incapable of creating any culture.
You can expect of us, as of a drunkard or thief anything at all..."[292]

Critics of Tertz's "conversion" from Communism to Christianity could say that he has simply substituted one "faith" for another
(an equation which he had made in his essay on socialist realism).
However, this would discount the basic contrast between the two
doctrines, the theoretical incompatibility between a teaching which
wants to create a paradise on earth, and another, which promises it
beyond this world. Tertz's basically Christian, completely anti-
materialistic, other-worldly attitude is nowhere as clearly revealed
as in his final major theme, the theme of death.

Life, according to Tertz, is like "an official business trip" — "short and full of responsibility." But "one cannot count on it as a steady domicile."[293] For the only, ultimate reality is death, which in its finality seems to outweigh the importance of life. And thus most of Tertz's "Thoughts" are concentrated on how to overcome the fear of death, how "to carry out the most important task in life — death,"[294] to the point of a definite death wish: "One should die in such a manner as to shout (whisper) before death: 'Hurrah! We are sailing away!'"[295]

From the literary point of view some of Tertz' formulations on death are rather interesting, as e.g. when he compares fear of death to cowardice on the battlefield, and goes on to encourage his imaginary partner: "Remember your cousin Verochka, who died at the age of 5? So tiny, and went away to die, suffocated by diptheria. And you, an adult, healthy, an educated man, you are afraid . . . Well, stop trembling! Be gay! Go on! March on!"[296] Or he compares the separation of body and soul in death to the work of a butcher who separates the meat from the bones. Or he sees man's fate "conceived in its ideal form in the genre of the tragedy which is played out in the direction of death."[297] The metaphor of sleep as a "rehearsal for death" is combined with the idea of its real "in-between" position, which permits actual communication with the dead (cf. the dream in "The Icicle"): "Sometimes (very rarely) the dead appear to us in dreams completely differently than usual people. That is, they speak and look as if they were alive, but this is not a dream of our former life with them, but a dream of our present meeting with them, who have suddenly come to life and have come to visit us . . ."[298]

Nothing can be worse than a "casual," debasing death, accordin to Tertz: "He lived, lived, and suddenly died."[299] And therefore he begs that fate may grant him "an honest, worthy death." Perhaps this strong orientation toward death, when one leaves behind all one's acquisitions — "knowledge, money, glory, works, books" — explains Tertz's disregard for personal safety in writing his "heretical" books. This is clearly restated in the following remark:

"Man lives in order to die. Death gives to life a plot-like direction (siuzhetnuiu napravlennost'), unity, certainty ... We subconsciously envy the completeness of the dead: they have already got out of the interim position, have acquired clearly defined characters, have lived their fill, have come to a final realization. Therefore we have such an interest for our *own* end ... We are attracted and seduced by suicide which permits us an advantageous deal ... But even more certain ... is to accept a death sentence with an announced verdict, which gives the victim the rare privilege of being present at its execution, and to realize oneself in true preparedness and completeness. Those who are condemned to death in one moment grow twice their size, and if they manage to preserve equanimity of spirit, it is difficult to imagine a better means of making the final calculation ..."[300]

These four major themes — body, soul, God, death, do not, of course, completely exhaust the content of the "Thoughts." There are some remarks on nature, which Tertz regards as the "prototype" of art, or the "visible form of eternity," and even some personal remarks, such as "All my life has been cowardice and supplication."[301] Yet these four themes form the basic canvas of Tertz's "Thoughts." Although there is no clear-cut philosophy behind them, there is a strong spiritual, even ascetic quality, a negation of the material in the widest sense of the word, traditionalism, and disbelief in the blessings of "progress." There is, of course, nothing new in what Tertz says. New is only the fact that what he says is being said in Soviet Russia, and that there emerges again the thirst for faith, the idealism, and the willingness for sacrifice that had characterized the best among the Russian intelligentsia of the 19th century.

Iulii Daniel' (Nikolai Arzhak): Biographical

Even less information than on Siniavskii is available on Iulii Daniel' who seems to have been virtually unknown until the time of his arrest. Born on November 15, 1925, the same year as Siniavskii, Daniel' comes apparently from an educated Jewish family. His father is presumed to have been the Yiddish short story writer, Mark Daniel' Meerovich who died in 1940. Despite his youth Daniel' participated actively in World War II, was severely wounded and received a pension after demobilization. He attended first Kharkov University, and then the Moscow Province Teachers' Training College, preparing for a career of school teaching. After completing his studies, he worked as a school teacher in the Kaluga province, and then in Moscow, but gave this up to become a poet-translator (from Yiddish, Caucasian and Slavic languages) — an ambition he had cherished since the age of 12. His translations seem to have been outstanding, judging by the complimentary inscriptions made for him by some of the authors.[302] One of his "legitimate" excursions into the realm of fiction writing had been a story entitled "Escape," which although printed never appeared for sale. Daniel' and Siniavskii probably became acquainted in the early 1950's when Daniel' moved to Moscow. In 1956 Siniavskii first read to him some of his "subversive" stories. Probably encouraged by his friend's example, and by the atmosphere of hope which followed the 20th Party Congress, Daniel' too began to write. His first tale, "The Hands," was written in 1956—57. This was followed by his best-known story, "This Is Moscow Speaking," which he wrote in 1960—61. "The Man from MINAP" was written in 1961, and "Atonement" in 1963. Using the same "channels" as Siniavskii (Mme. Peltier-Zamoiska and her French connections) he sent his stories abroad, where they were published under the pseudonym of Nikolai Arzhak.

Compared to the colorful, extremely complex, and quite prolific (considering the short time span available to him) Tertz, Arzhak appears much less spectacular. His output is small. There is no theoretical background to his stories as was the case with Tertz. It is further interesting to note that all four of Arzhak's stories were used by the prosecution as evidence of their author's "anti-Soviet" attitude (whereas only three out of Tertz's ten stories were similarly cited). This brings out the basic difference between the two writers. Although Arzhak too is not a "socialist realist" (his stories lacking positive heroes, Purpose-oriented plots, and official optimism), although he occasionally resorts to fantasy, fantastic satire and symbolism, he is more of a traditional realist than is Tertz. All his stories are time-bound, in the sense of being tied to definite historical periods, trends, or milieus. Soviet reality is always the basis for his stories, and his unequivocal, ironic treatment of certain aspects of this reality makes it relatively easy to interpret (or misinterpret) him. However, Arzhak is not only a chronicler of Soviet *byt* as were Zoshchenko and Il'f and Petrov. Reality is for him but the starting point for excursions into human psychology (of marginal importance in Tertz), and ultimately into moral, ethical questions. There is an intensity of feeling, of personal involvement, even suffering in Arzhak which brings him closer to the generation of young Soviet "realists" (Aksenov, Kazakov) who advocate "sincerity" in writing, rather than to the ironically detached theoretician of a new, phantasmagoric art. Finally, and again in contrast to Tertz, there is a very clear, poetic strain in Arzhak, probably a reflection of his activity as a translator of poetry. There are about 15 poems of various lenghts, attributed to fictitious authors (e.g. Il'ia Chur), or fictional characters in "This Is Moscow Speaking," and "Atonement." These poems, mostly intentionally obscure in meaning, often unusual in the choice of vocabulary and rhyme, seem like imitations of "modern" poetry, also frowned upon by the proponents of socialist realism. To give only one example:

> They lie in hiding in every doorway,
> They rise with the smell of carbolic acid,
> They are in the grass, growing from the soil,
> In old books, slumbering on the shelf.
> Everywhere a lifeless whisper is heard,
> And every phrase conceals a bad ending.
> They are in the water, streaming in the shower,
> And in the bold muttering of the lavatory pan.

Georgii Bolotin, "The Demons of Death"
(in chapter 5, "This Is Moscow Speaking")

Arzhak's Work

1. "The Hands" ("Ruki"), 1956—57

Arzhak earliest story is, as he testified at the trial, "a literary recording of a real occurence."[303] Extremely short (about 5 pages), it is presented in the "skaz" form, as one part of a dialogue between the narrator (identified later on as Vasilii Malinin, a simple factory worker), and a silent listener, Sergei, "an intellectual" as Malinin calls him, and former comrade in arms during the Revolution. Meeting after a lengthy period of time, Malinin wants to explain to his listener the reason why his hands are shaking and have become virtually useless for work: "Our guys at the factory, they say directly: 'Hey, they say, Vas'ka, have you drunk yourself silly?' (dopilsia do ruchki)-[a pun] ... This, my friend, is not from drink ..."[304] And Malinin then proceeds to tell his story, presented as a flash-back to the early 1920's, which vividly recreates the atmosphere of that period (as seen through the eyes of a simple man), and eventually poses a moral question which the narrator seemingly, however, does not understand.

Malinin, a loyal Bolshevik and Party member during the Revolution, is suddenly drafted into the Cheka, "to fight the counter-revolution," and to execute "enemies of the state." He accepts the assignment as a matter of course, and carries out his duties to the best of his abilities. "The work (rabotenka) is not exactly hard, but you can't call it light either. It affects the heart," Malinin reminisces. "Of course," he adds parenthetically, "they gave us vodka ... You can't [manage] otherwise ..."[305]

The crisis in Malinin's soul occurs when he is ordered to execute several priests whose guilt is not even clear to Malinin: "They were stirring up their parishioners. Because of Tikhon, probably. Or in general, against socialism — I don't know. But to put it clearly — they were enemies ..."[306] So far Malinin had been able to kill because he felt no association with his victims. But with priests it is different. "Not that I was afraid, or attached to religion," he tells. "No, I am a Party man, firm, I don't believe in all this folly — various gods, angels, and archangels . . ."[307] But there were childhood reminiscences of how his mother used to take him to the village church, how he used to kiss the hand of the priest whose name was also Vasilii. He tries to overcome his "weakness," and manages to shoot two priests, even though he feels violently sick in the interval. When he leads out the third priest, a handsome young man, he is quite uneasy, and even talks to his victim, which he had never done before. Then he shoots him in the back. But the priest does not fall as expected, and instead turns around and walks toward his executioner, cursing him and glorifying God. Malinin shoots several times at close range, but the priest remains unharmed. "He stands before me, his eyes are blazing like a wolfe's, his breast is bare, and a sort of radiance comes from his head . . . 'Your hands are bloody', he shouts, 'look at your hands!'"[308] Malinin runs away in terror, collapses, and has a nervous breakdown. After recovering in a hospital he is discharged from the Cheka, for his hands keep shaking from that time on. Was it a miracle that he had witnessed? No, it turns out that Malinin's comrades had played a prank on him by putting blank cartridges into his rifle before the third execution.

The most distinctive feature of the story is its language — a mixture of low, colloquial Russian and Soviet slogans of the time, reflecting clearly the influence of Zoshchenko. The comical naiveté of the narration forms a grotesque contrast to the gloominess of its contents. Thus Malinin tells of his mobilization into the Cheka as follows: "I had worked [at the factory] not more than a year when, bang, they call me to the Regional Committee (raikom). 'Here,' they say, 'Malinin, is an order (putevka) for you. The Party, they say, mobilizes you, Malinin, Vasilii Semenovich, into the ranks of the valorous Extraordinary Commission (Cherezvychainaia kommissia, Cheka, for short), to fight the counter-revolution. We wish you, they say, success in the fight with the world bourgeoisie, and give our humble regards to comrade Dzerzhinskii, if you see him.'"[309] The retelling of the allegorical speech of Feliks Dzerzhinskii (the notorious head of the Cheka) to the newly enlisted men is, despite its ominous message, also comical: "... he had us line up in a row, and said that you can't build a house on a moor, it is necessary, he said, to dry out the moor first, and that thereby, he said, it is necessary to annihilate all sorts of toads and vipers, for that, he said, is an iron necessity. And to this, he said, each has to lend his hand . . ."[310] This successful brainwashing is clearly reflected in Malinin's thoughts during executions: "You walk behind him [the victim] along the yard, and you think and say to yourself: 'It is necessary, Vasilii, NECESSARY. If you don't finish him off, he the viper, will immediately destroy the whole Soviet republic.'"[311]

Another important feature in "The Hands" is the subtle portrayal of the psychology of a simple man. And what Arzhak reveals here is the same element which Tertz had shown in "At the Circus," and especially in *Liubimov:* the persistence of religious "prejudices," of a religious undercurrent in the minds of simple people that cannot be eradicated, and which inevitably lead to a conflict with Communism. Despite Malinin's unquestionable loyalty to the new regime, despite his naive belief in the necessity of the executions, and his matter-of-fact attitude toward them, he is ultimately broken in this conflict. "Shoot me, I say, Feliks Edmundych," he shouts at Dzerzhinskii after his terrifying experience, "I cannot kill a priest!"[312]

And finally, beyond this psychological portrayal, Arzhak raises a clear, moral question in the story: Is one justified to kill for the sake of an idea? The answer to this is implied, even though not

clearly stated. It is in the next story, "This Is Moscow Speaking,"
that Arzhak gives an unequivocal reply to that question.

2. "This Is Moscow Speaking" ("Govorit Moskva"), 1960—61

Arzhak's next story, in terms of chronology, is his most striking
and original tale. In its strong political impact it is reminiscent of
Tertz's "The Trial Begins," even though it lacks the latter's complex
philosophical framework. And in its own, though different way,
"This Is Moscow Speaking" is another example of the "many-
layeredness" of modern Russian (uncensored) fiction. On one level,
it is pure grotesque fantasy.[313] On another, it presents a picture of
Soviet life, as well as of Soviet political reality as Arzhak saw it:
"In 1960—61, when the story was written, I and not I alone, but
anyone who seriously considered the state of affairs in our country,
was convinced that it was on the verge of establishing a second,
new cult of personality. Not too much time had passed since the
death of Stalin. We all remembered well what was termed 'violation
of socialist legality'. And now I saw again all the symptoms: again
one person dictated his will to the agronomists, artists, diplomats,
and writers. We saw how once again from the pages of newspapers
and posters flashed one name, and how again the most crude and
banal utterings of this man were presented to us as a revelation,
as the quintessence of wisdom . . ." Arzhak stated at his trial.[314] But
the fear of renewed terror inspired by the "Khrushchev era" (un-
founded, as seen retrospectively) is not the main point of the story,
just as the fantastic hypothesis posed in it is only an artistic device.
Arzhak's main concerns are human behavior, human psychology,
and beyond this, eternal moral questions. What would happen in a
totalitarian state, if the government were to announce suddenly a
monstrous ordinance, such as a "Day of Public Murders?" he asks.

Would there be any opposition to it on the part of the population? Would there be a revolt? And finally, as in "The Hands" he poses the question: Is killing permissible?

The answers given by Arzhak are, essentially, pessimistic: people in totalitarian societies have become so passive and fearful that their official reaction is apathy, while their private thoughts are concerned only with personal safety and survival. As to the last question, Arzhak replies with a clear "Thou shalt not kill!" and the story — the only one among Arzhak's tales — ends on a vague note of hope. For there may be a few individuals, such as the narrator, Anatolii Kartsev, who will have the courage to stand up, to refuse intimidation, and to act according to their conscience. And it is those people through whom the real voice of Moscow, and of the real Russia are speaking.

The story, which consists of 8 chapters, narrated in the first person form as a flash-back by its hero, is set in Moscow and embraces a relatively short period of time (July to November), with August 10, 1960 forming the high-point of the action. This concentration in time, unity of place, and the absence of sub-plots contribute to an atmosphere of tension and suspense which dominates the tale. The beginning of the action is dated July 16, and starts in a very realistic, low key: a week-end get-together by a group of friends, middle-aged Muscovite intellectuals at a *dacha* near Moscow. Against the peaceful background of an early Sunday morning suddenly explodes an official radio announcement about a proposed "Day of Public Murders":

"... On that day any citizen of the Soviet Union who has reached the age of 16 has the right to murder freely any other citizen with the exception of persons mentioned in paragraph 1 of the addendum to the present ordinance. The ordinance will be effective from 6 A. M. to 12 P. M. Moscow time. August 10, 1960.

Addendum: 1. It is prohibited to murder a) children under 16 years of age, b) military and militia personnel in uniform, c) transport workers on duty.

2. Murders committed prior or subsequent to the above mentioned date and with the intent of robbery, or as a consequence of rape will be considered criminal offenses, and will be punished in accordance with the existing laws. Moscow. The Kremlin. The Chairman of the Supreme Presidium . . ."[315]

While no one present understands the meaning of the grotesque ordinance (". . . It's a provocation. It must be the 'Voice of America'," says one of those present; "I believe they are plotting something against the Jews," says another who is Jewish), the mentality produced by a totalitarian regime manifests itself only too clearly. It does not occur to anyone to feel outraged, to protest, or to take any action. Instead, the holiday mood, and even the harmony among the friends is temporarily disrupted, and as "the Day" draws closer (chapters 2-6) each of them goes his own way, trying to accomodate himself to it as best as possible. Some, as e.g. Igor', one of the narrator's friends, repeat Party slogans to the effect that the ordinance is "the result of the wise policies of our Party." Others, like Volodia Margulis, a Jew, keeps a gun swearing that "they" won't get him easily. Still others try to gain some profit from it. Thus Sasha Chuprov, a "liberal" painter who is unable to sell his pictures "tainted by the pernicious influence of the West," nevertheless paints a propaganda poster for "the Day." (Paradoxically, it is rejected for its alleged modernism, and suitability for "Life" magazine). And Kartsev's mistress Zoia even seriously considers the licence of the day for murdering her elderly, boring husband.

The "Day" itself, as seen through the eyes of the narrator proves factually anti-climactic.[316] Most people hide in their rooms and apartments, and only a few — the young, the Party-minded, the curious — venture out into the streets. Kartsev, who goes out after a grave struggle with himself, encounters death twice: in the form of an unknown corpse lying in the Arbat square, and in the person of an unknown, zealous citizen who tries to murder him right in front of the Lenin Mausoleum, but fails. The final chapter (8) finds the friends happily reunited at a party held on the occasion of the October Revolution, most of them having already forgotten, or trying not to remember "the Day." It is only the narrator, Anatolii Kartsev, who goes through a spiritual crisis during this period, and emerges deeply chastened from his experience.

The figure of Kartsev is central to the story. Through him Arzhak shows the whole life-style, feelings and attitudes of a certain group of people (middle-aged, Soviet intellectuals), while at the same time bringing the psychological and moral problems of "the Day" into especially clear and dramatic focus. Finally, there can also be no doubt that Kartsev is a partial emanation of his author, both in terms of biographical features (age, the war record, literary work and interests) as well as ideological attitudes (patriotism, civic courage), even though Arzhak tries to stress his complete ordinariness.

A typical representative of the "younger" generation to whom the Stalin era is only a childhood memory, Kartsev, a veteran of World War II (in which he was severely wounded) is working in a government publishing house since his return to private life. Although he stresses the fact that he is neither a writer nor a graphomaniac, he has definite literary inclinations. His notes serve not only the purpose of recapitulating the past (August 10), but are also a safety valve so important in a totalitarian society: "If I feel like writing e.g. 'And the piano like black African shows its tooth in a negroid manner' I will do so. Nobody will accuse me of pretentiousness or colonialism."[317] Finally, there is also a clear authorial

echo in his feelings that it is not "very pretty" to be published
abroad (even if it is impossible to publish the notes in Soviet
Russia), and in his hope that in "many, many years' time" someone
may read them.

In his political attitudes Kartsev tends to be "neutral," his
indifference being partly the result of a "trauma" (the terror of the
30's to which his father, a convinced Communist, fell victim),
partly to his feeling that the present rulers have perverted the
ideals of the Russian Revolution. "If I feel like writing about the
government that they are all demagogues, hypocrites, and scum in
general, I'll write even that," he notes. "I can permit myself the
luxury of being a Communist in private."[318] Yet he is obviously
not an anti-Communist, but rather an "ideal" Communist who has
been disappointed by the reality around him. Feeling provoked by
Volodia Margulis's anti-government jokes, Kartsev insists that one
must defend "the real Soviet power," and there seems to be no
doubt in his mind as to the rightness of the Revolution. "People of
my generation have no right to blabber about those times," he says.
"My father was a commissar during the Civil War, and I think he
knew what he was fighting for."[319]

In his private life, on the other hand, Kartsev can hardly be
termed idealistic. A bachelor at 35, he loves poetry, drink and
women, takes life easily and avoids complications or commitments
of any sort. His liaison with Zina reflects not only the relaxation of
traditional moral standards in contemporary Soviet Russia
(carefully purged from official literature), but also his own, modern
approach to sex. "No, I look at all these things in a simpler manner,"
he says to himself while listening to the love-woes of a friend.
"From the very beginning there should be no games, no diplomacy,
no obligations, so that everything is honest. Do we like each other?
Wonderful. Do we want each other? Great. What else is there?
Marital infidelity? Adultery? So what?"[320]

Kartsev's reaction to the announcement of "the Day" is at first the same as everybody else's — he tries not to think about it and follows his usual occupation. An editorial in "Izvestiia" filled with the usual obtuse clichés gives certain reassurance. There had been "Days of the Artillery," "Days of the Soviet Press," so that a "Day of Public Murders" must be similar. It is only when Kartsev is forced to face the issue of murder squarely that his previous complacency is profoundly shaken, and a different "self" begins to manifest itself. The first jolt comes from Zina. "Let's kill Pavlik," she casually suggests while lying in bed with him. "There won't be another occasion like that. I have figured it all out . . ."[321] Kartsev's indignant refusal, taken by her as a sign of cowardice, sets a whole train of thoughts in motion in his mind. Going back in his memory from his university days to the war experience he tries to find anyone whom he would want to kill out of a feeling of vengeance — and finds none. Another jolt — fear for his own life that might be threatened by some unknown enemy — comes after an encounter with Arbatov, an old man, who points to the irrational (rather than pragmatic) source of murder. ". . . I do not want to kill, and cannot kill, but others may wish to and be capable of doing so," Kartsev realizes. It is this fear which, rising to a crescendo (and expressed in an interesting, literary stream-of-consciousness manner) forms the psychological highpoint of the story: "I will hide, I will barricade myself, I will sit it out in my room." Kartsev thinks. "I do not want to die, I do n-o-t w-a-n-t to! . . . If they burst into the room, I will beat them like dogs with a crowbar. Better a live dog. Recently I was at a dog show. I very much liked the greyhounds — with narrow, long heads that look like duelling pistols. And could I fight a duel? Pushkin's bullet hit Dantes' button. If I go out on Sunday [the Day"] I'll have to put my cigarette case into the breast pocket of my jacket, left where the heart is. 'Left Where the Heart Is' — that's a novel by Leonhard Frank, very boring. And Bruno

Frank — that's something entirely different, he wrote a book on Cervantes. And what would Don Quixote have done on August 10? He would ride around Moscow on his Rocinante and defend everyone. On his personal Rocinante. The crank with a copper pan on his head, he would ride over Red Square, ready to break his lance in the name of the Beautiful Lady, in the name of Russia . . ."[322]

And finally overcoming his fear, Kartsev like a modern Don Quixote decides to go out into the streets on "the Day," facing danger and possible death. "A Pontius Pilate who is betraying his own soul every day — what am I worth?" he asks himself. And he decides that he cannot let "them" kill him morally, and thus preserve his own life. "Wait, what shall I do? I will go out into the streets the day after tomorrow and will shout: 'Citizens, don't kill each other! Love thy neighbor!' . . . Whom will I save? I don't know. I don't know anything . . . Perhaps I will save myself. If it is not too late . . ."[323] Kartsev does save himself by the simple act of not letting himself be intimidated. His only dangerous encounter with the zealot who tries to kill him, is anti-climactic and grotesque, taking place at the Communist "holy of holies" — the Lenin Mausoleum, with an impassionate sentry watching the scuffle. And despite fear and disaffection. Kartsev's narrative ends on a strong patriotic and moral note: "I believe that that which I have written could have been written by any other man of my generation, my fate, who loves this accursed, this beautiful country as I do. I judged it and its people and myself better and worse than I should have. But who will reproach me for that?" And he says to himself: "This is your world, your life, and you are a cell, a part of it. You must not let [them] frighten you. You have to answer for yourself, and through this you are responsible for others."[324] It seems very likely that Kartsev's profession of faith reflects the feelings of his author.

The narrator's psychological struggle between fear and civic courage is enhanced by the motif of fear which runs through the narrative. Its origin lies both in the past (the Stalin era), and the future (the possibilities implied by "the Day"). Looking at the modern buildings of Moscow standing right next to those of the 30's, Kartsev is apprehensive of the future, if another Stalin were to arise. As "the Day" draws nearer, the narrator notes that people "in the subway, at the movies, in the streets ... went up to others, and smiling in an ingratiating manner began to talk about their illnesses, about fishing, about the quality of nylon stockings — in short, about anything at all. And if they were not shut up immediately, and listened to, they for a long time shook the hand of their listener, gratefully and soul-searchingly looking into their eyes."[325]

The most pathetic example of this universal fear occurs on "the Day" when the narrator collides with an elderly neighbor on the stairs of his apartment building, the latter taking his attempts to help her for attempts at murder: "... She screamed, dashed to the side, the net with bottles hit the railing. Glass splintered, kefir gushed through the holes of the net onto the landing ... I rushed to help her. And here she screamed for the second time, and closing her eyes, began weakly to push me away with trembling hands '... Tolia, Tolia,' she muttered incoherently, 'I [knew] you when you were little ... in my arms ... I [knew] your mother. Tolia!'"[326]

The fantastic and grotesque aspects of the story are counter-balanced by a matter-of-fact, ironic style. Although the figure of the narrator dominates the tale, there are some secondary characters, presented with only a few, ironic strokes, who contribute to making "This Is Moscow Speaking" a convincing panorama of Soviet life. There is Kartsev's neighbor in the communal apartment who despite having been a political prisoner is an eloquent apologist of government policies: "... The present ordinance is nothing else but the logical continuation of a process that has already started — the process of democratization. Democratization of what? Democratization of the organs of executive power. The ideal, however, understand me correctly, is the gradual dissolution of the executive powers in the broad popular masses, at the very bottom, so to speak. That is, not at the bottom, I did not express myself correctly, how could we have a bottom, well, you understand me . . ."[327] he rambles on while washing the dishes in the communal kitchen. There is Volodia Margulis, passively hostile to the regime, who despite being married, engages in "difficult" love affairs on the side. Zina, Kartsev's mistress, beautiful but devoid of any moral inhibitions is a typical Soviet "bourgeois" whose ideals are personal comfort and welfare (cf. Marina in "The Trial Begins"). More interesting than all these "new" people, however, is an old man, Arbatov with whom Kartsev spends one evening. Arbatov's neat room, his orderly manner, formality of speech (he insists on the use of the patronymic) reflect the order and self-discipline of an earlier generation. Hiding his spirituality behind the mask of simplicity, just as he hides his huge library behind a heavy, grey curtain, Arbatov evokes the image of a different, old, nearly extinct Russia. And it is perhaps symbolic that he commits suicide on "the Day of Public Murders."

Besides these characters there are various fragmentary observations, comments and allusions to Soviet life which further contribute to the "realism" of "This Is Moscow Speaking." There are e. g. references to Soviet art and its rejection of modernism, to anti-Semitism which continues to thrive, to problems with Union Republics where ordinances from the center are not always carried out, to housing shortages which hinder but do not prevent love affairs, and so on.

Arzhak's ear is as keen as is his eye. He reproduces with brilliant irony the official Soviet jargon, as e.g. in the "explanation" to the "Day of Public Murders" given by "Izvestiia": "The growing welfare — gigantic steps — real democracy — only in our country all thoughts — for the first time in history — visible signs — bourgeois press . . ."[328] The same attention to language can also be observed in the language of the narrator and his friends, which gives a vivid picture of contemporary Soviet Russian of the younger generation, its colloquialism, sub-standard, and newly-coined expressions.

In contrast to Tertz, Arzhak's stylistic devices are, with a few exceptions, rather traditional and realistic. Each chapter of the story has a poetic epigraph attributed to various authors (Il'ia Chur, Kirill Zamoiskii, Georgii Bolotin, Richard O'Hara), although there can be no doubt that their author is Arzhak himself. These poems or epigraphs not only refer to the action in the individual chapters, they also seem to underline the main ideas of the story. Thus the poem "Moscow Boulevards" (chapter 1) underlines man's helplessness versus life through the figure of a young, stray cat. The poem "Tickets for Sale" (chapter 2) — one of the most interesting in the story — speaks of the necessity of wearing masks in (Soviet) life, since it would be unbearable otherwise:

> Well, who could stand it, who could tolerate it,
> If there were no sale of masks
> For us, to be taken home,
> For each day, each hour?
> Put on the costume of an elevator man, and a poet,
> Of an enthusiast and a fop.
> Knock at the window for a ticket,
> Shout! But do not forget thereby
> That "Admission without masks is forbidden."

The theme of death — so dominant in the story — is expressed in the poems to chapters 4, 5, 6. Finally, a parallel between "the Day" and the day of Last Judgement is drawn in the poem, "To You Poets," preceding chapter 7.

Only occasionally does Arzhak attempt to use a "surrealist" technique of fragmentary ideas, phrases, images, as e.g. in chapter 4 when the narrator has a vision of his war experience: "... There they lie torn into shreds by an explosion, cut up by bullets. It's slippery, one's feet slip. Who is this? He crawls, dragging after him his intestines along the inlaid floor covered with plaster. Ah, it is he, covered with medals who accompanied the Chief on trains! Why is he skinny? Why is there a quilted coat on him? I already saw him once, as he crawled along the greider, having thrown out the redness and blueness of his stomach onto the dust ..."[329]

One of the most elaborate metaphors in the story occurs at the moment when Arbatov opens the grey curtain which hid his library from his visitors. And it is interesting that literature here is shown as being unable to provide an absolute truth, to help man in his moral dilemmas: "Many-colored, bound in flowery cottons, the writers dashed into the room like a Tatar horde, tearing into pieces the appearance of well-being, the deceitful calm of a bourgeois comfort, and with it — the creaky, huge carts of philosophical systems, the crooked mirrors of the sabres of self-analysis, the dull battering rams of universal pessimism, the stallions of civilization with the yellow foam of misanthropy on their bared muzzles, who trampled to pieces, to flat cakes the greyhaired Evangelists who raised toward the indifferent ceiling their Commands which were turning into atomic dust ..."[330]

A vivid mosaic of life — this is the background of the psychological and moral problems raised by "This Is Moscow Speaking."

3. "The Man from MINAP" ("Chelovek iz MINAPa"), 1961

This relatively short story is the only example of the lighter side in Arzhak. Although the writer treats an essentially serious

problem — the conflict between Soviet law and Party interests —
he presents it in the form of a highly amusing satire on Soviet
scientific "discoveries,"[331] while at the same time painting an ironic
picture of Soviet society and its mores. The motif of supernatural
powers, suddenly acquired by the hero (as in Tertz's "The Icicle,"
written at about the same time) is used here on a risqué, erotic, but
rather funny level. What would happen to a man who would
violate the (Victorian) Soviet moral code, but whose "immoral"
activity may be useful to the state, Arzhak asks. The answer is,
of course, predictable, since questions of morality become relative
and flexible in a totalitarian state where Party interests are the
supreme dictate.

Presented in 7 short chapters by an anonymous narrator who
only rarely intrudes into the tale, the story tells of the fate of
Volodia Zalesskii, a student at the Moscow Institute of Scientific
Profanation (sic!) who becomes a victim of circumstances and of
his very special talents. The setting of the story is again primarily
Moscow, with the plot being developed retrospectively: from the
time when the first meeting between the hero and Vera Ivanovna
Krants took place in the Crimea 3 years earlier (chapter 3).
Through Vera Ivanovna Arzhak paints the portrait of the new
Soviet bourgeoisie (just as he presented the "new" intelligentsia in
"This Is Moscow Speaking") which is as pleasure loving and
materialistic as the latter. Marital fidelity is hardly an issue, and
during vacations people "loved diligently, not sparing themselves,
putting into this measure all the working enthusiasm which [they]
had not expended on work."[332] Although married to an attentive,
well-earning Jewish husband, and mother of a charming boy of 4,
Vera Ivanovna starts an affair with Volodia. In a moment of
drunken intimacy, Volodia confides to his mistress that he is able
to determine the sex of a child at the moment of conception by an
effort of his will. Although incredulous at first, Vera Ivanovna

who is anxious to have a daughter, makes use of Volodia's capacities in due time and with the proper results, (her husband, Semen
Moiseevich, remaining of course blissfully unaware of his doubtful
paternity). But being "civic-minded" and "selfless" Vera Ivanovna
feels that Volodia has no right to hide such a marvellous talent,
and exhorts him to do his duty in regard to other, less fortunate
families. Volodia agrees, and soon finds himself in heavy demand
by various frustrated Soviet wives who cannot obtain similarly
reliable services from their legal spouses.

The crisis occurs when Volodia is caught *in flagranti* with a
friend of Vera Ivanovna, Anna L'vovna, whose husband had
always insisted on a male heir, but who cannot quite comprehend
his wife's selflessness in the given situation. Volodia is hauled
before an open Komsomol meeting, with a view of being expelled
from the Komsomol as well as the Institute. The scene of the
meeting (chapter 5) forms the highpoint of the story, and is a
masterful parody on Soviet "show" trials, in which the verdict has
been reached already beforehand. Volodia is subjected to severe
attacks by various members of the Institute, and despite his
attempts to explain the situation, he seems to be doomed. But at
that point the Party secretary suddenly has an inspired idea and
closes the proceedings.

Volodia is brought to the notice of high Party officials and
medical experts. His record and his methods are carefully in-
vestigated to determine whether they are compatible with Marxist
ideology. It is only now that Volodia's "secret" is revealed which,
as becomes evident, is firmly grounded on "pure dialectics." For
having been told as a child that children are produced by an effort
of will, and possessing besides an extraordinary photographic
memory, he had at his first intercourse visualized the portrait of
Karl Marx, "the founder of scientific socialism." The result —
a boy — encouraged him to experiment further, with equally

reliable results. If he wanted to produce a girl, he visualized Klara
Zetkin; if he wanted twins, he would evoke a double image of
Marx or of Zetkin, or Marx/Zetkin. As a result of this screening,
and the obvious proofs Volodia from an accused suddenly becomes
a hero, entrusted to train other Soviet men to be as proficient as
he is.

Unfortunately, however, Volodia's talent proves to be unique
"like the talent of Paganini." The hopes of high Soviet officials
and geneticists for a revolutionary transformation of biological
processes is frustrated. Volodia is put in a prisonlike villa, where
he "eats, sleeps, exercises and watches television under the super-
vision of doctors" (somewhat like the hero in "The Icicle"), and is
utilized only in narrow, and presumably high, Party circles. He
lives well, but is bored, and bothered by the fact that he will
remain without a profession, once he should lose his miraculous
talent.

As can be seen from the plot outline, the story is a farce and
there is no attempt at introducing any psychological description
or problematics. The hero, Volodia, is less a personality than a
passive receptacle of a strange talent which he does not even much
care about. He is no Don Juan, and his complete disinterestedness
in sex is strinkingly evident in the piquant description of his first
relations with Anna L'vovna: "In the bedroom he took her by both
breasts in a business-like manner as if weighing them. Then he
turned Anna L'vovna round, and opened the buttons on the back
of her dress. This ended the period of courting. He let go of her,
took off his jacket, looked for a hanger, and not finding one, put
it on the back of a chair. Taking off his pants, he turned around
and in an absent-minded way looked at Anna L'vovna. 'Well?' he
said . . ." At the end of the story there is something pathetic
in the picture of the de-humanized Volodia who no longer bears
a name, but is only referred to as "the man from MINAP." Equally

sketchy are Vera Ivanovna, Anna L'vovna, and even her husband who turns "the color of the complete collected works of V. I. Lenin (not the 3rd but the 4th edition)"[334] when he finds Volodia in bed with his wife.

What Arzhak emphasizes in the story is clearly the farcical character of Soviet judicial standards (which he was to experience personally), and the pressures put upon scientists by the Party leadership to produce new, sensational discoveries in order to bolster the image of Soviet science in the world. Both these features are well brought out in chapter 5 (the Komsomol meeting), and chapter 6 (a high Party meeting). Arzhak's satiric method in describing these two scenes is primarily through reproducing the language of the persons involved, a "tape-recorder" method, rather than through physical descriptions or commentaries by the author. The scene of the Komsomol meeting starts with the reading of the letter by the plaintiff, Leonid Nikolaevich Kniazhitskii, (Anna L'vovna's husband) which in its semi-literate naiveté, and use of official chlichés is highly amusing:

"... The aforenamed Zalesskii, Vladimir Al'bertovich, was found by me on Wednesday, March 17 of this year at 13 hours 30 minutes Moscow time, in my personal apartment, at the moment when he violated (narushil) my marital fidelity with my wife, Kniazhitskaia, Anna L'vovna. As a member of the Party since 1949 I cannot bypass the ugly fact that citizen Zalesskii was supposed to be at that moment at a lecture on the political economics of socialism, which is confirmed by the schedule of lectures in the vestibule of your Institute ... And in addition to all this my wife, who soon will be an ex-wife, confessed that citizen Zalesskii had violated her marital fidelity for the second time, and the first time he did it at the apartment of her friend, Krants, Vera Ivanovna, whose husband is engaged in shady dealings on the supply branch, while eating Russian lard ..."[335]

This letter which evokes general amusement is followed by a blasting speech by a venerable Academician who appeals to the moral instincts of the assembly, and accuses Zalesskii of "alien ideology" and false pretenses for his Don Juanish behavior. For if "the most progressive science in the world, Soviet science" cannot regulate the sex of a child, how can he do that, the professor exclaims. A Komsomol member then points to Zalesskii's "alien" image — "Moustache! Nylon shirt! Narrow pants! And what is hidden behind these narrow pants?"[336] — and demands the immediate expulsion of Zalesskii from the Komsomol.

While all this goes on, the Party secretary of the Institute, Dmitrii Ivanovich Bronin, debates within himself as to what to say and what course of action to take. This is presented in a rather funny stream-of-consciousness method, in which Bronin's official and private thoughts intermingle: ". . . At the time when the Party and all our community devote maximum attention to the strengthening of the Soviet family — that Kniazhitskaia is not bad-looking at all — the action of the Komsomol member Zalesskii is in blatant contradiction to all ethical norms — how does he do that, in hell's name?! . . . Repeating the ridiculous lie about his supernatural abilities, Zalesskii is pouring water on the mill of idealists, contributes to the spread of prejudice, undermines faith in the correctness of science, and in the final analysis, carries out ideological diversion! — didn't do too badly: the women fed him, gave him booze; probably he got some money too? — I am sure that Zalesskii had also a material, monetary interest: these types are not squeamish, and I gave that slut 50 rubles . . .[337] Finally, deciding that Zalesskii may be worth investigating, Bronin makes a quick call to his superior and closes the meeting.

The conversation in the High Party Committee (chapter 6), with a mysterious chief Pavel Petrovich, his subordinates comrades Volkov, and Trofim Denisovich, and a famous professor, is a marvellous piece of satire, reminiscent of the Party meeting in *Liubimov*. While the professor has no scientific explanation for Zalesskii's marvellous capabilities, the high Party command already develops a whole program: "... We have to approach this economically, prudently. The first thing to find out is whether he will be able to teach others. If he does, then we can go over to planned childbearing. We have to get exact firgures on the production of clothing, shoes, bras and ladies' bikes. In the course of 18-20 years the difference in the number of women and men has to be eliminated. So that each would have according to need. As to the unmarried — they will be put on trial. Is it right, what I am saying, comrades?[338] There is no question of discussion, of "collective leadership," and everything is settled there and then.

"The Man from MINAP" is not a very profound work, and somewhere perhaps just on the borderline of good taste. Yet its political satire, its "acoustic" qualities (the "ear" which Arzhak has for speech) counterbalances its artistic deficiencies, and makes it a refreshing piece of writing.

4. "Atonement" ("Iskuplenie"), 1963

Arzhak's last story is his longest and perhaps even the best among his four tales. Although less obvious in stating its problematics than "This Is Moscow Speaking" it is in some ways a more serious and mature work. It shows Arzhak's continued deep preoccupation with moral, ethical problems, and an interesting evolution of style in the direction of fantasy and symbolism.

"Atonement" can be regarded as a counterpart to "This Is Moscow Speaking." It is again a tale which moves on various levels — a political, psychological, and moral. Arzhak portrays the same milieu — Muscovite middle-aged intellectuals, — similar attitudes and mores which he had shown in the earlier story. Finally, the

narrator-hero, Viktor Vol'skii, seems to be only a slight variation
of Anatolii Kartsev. However, this time there is no fantastic
outward trial (like "the Day of Public Murders") which confronts
the hero. Rather, it is a problem from "within," that he has to face,
a crisis against which he has no defenses, and which makes his final
ruin both pityful and tragic.

The story which consists of 12[339] short chapters narrated in the
first person form by the hero, is set in the relatively "liberal" and
relaxed early 60's, and covers a short period of time (summer to
fall, 1963), with only a few flash-backs to the narrator's childhood
(chapter 3), and his war-time experiences (chapter 5): the whole
intellectual atmosphere has changed for the better; there is more
contact with and information on the cultural life of the West; in
intimate circles people discuss philosophical and moral questions
and recite poetry. Even the "decadent" Gipsy song tradition has
been revived and is nearly acceptable. The horrors of the Stalin-era
— only a decade removed — seem to have been completely
forgotten by a "clean, washed, and well-eating intelligentsia" which
has been personally spared hardship. Echoes of the past come only
through the songs of former camp inmates (many of them returning
from Siberia under the amnesty) which had become nearly as
fashionable as the Gipsy songs.

Again, as in "This Is Moscow Speaking," the narrator of the
tale is a typical representative of these relatively carefree, unsuffer-
ing people, and of this particular intellectual climate and attitudes.
37 years old, unmarried, a painter-artist working in a government
agency producing posters (although doing also some "real" painting
on the side) Viktor Vol'skii has survived the 30's and the dangers of
World War II. The war in which he was wounded and saw human
suffering awakened in him a desire for self-preservation: "It was
perhaps then that for the first time it came to my mind that it is
easier to die than to be in prison. Perhaps it was exactly from that

time on that I began to be more careful in conversations, safeguard-
ing my freedom. Freedom? Yes, freedom: I painted, I drank wine,
I swam in the sea, I caressed women . . ."[340]

Like Kartsev, Vol'skii is jolted out of his complacent, self-
centered existence and forced to a reevaluation of all his former
values. But this jolt is quite undramatic and accidental. Trying to
while away time before a rendez-vous with Irina — the girl with
whom he is in love — Vol'skii notices a man staring fixedly at him
in the foyer of a movie house. Before Vol'skii has a chance to speak
to him the man disappears. A second, accidental meeting between
Vol'skii and the stranger occurs in a small circle of Vol'skii's friends,
where the latter turns out to be an acquaintance of the hostess,
identified as Feliks Chernov. In a flashback Vol'skii remembers
him as a co-student in the early 50's (i.e. the early fall of 1951, the
last year of Stalin's rule) whom he had subsequently lost sight of.
But his attempts at renewing his acquaintance with Chernov meet a
strange hostility and rejection on the latter's part. When, on
Vol'skii's insistence, they finally meet, Chernov tells him that he
had spent years in concentration camps on charges of "anti-Soviet
propaganda," and that by logic of elimination it could have been
only Vol'skii who denounced him. He demands that Vol'skii
disappear from Moscow and go into voluntary exile in the Far East
or Central Asia — else he would destroy his reputation and make
it impossible for him to have any human contacts.

Before Vol'skii has a chance to justify himself, Chernov
disappears. And although Vol'skii knows that he never denounced
Chernov nor anybody else, he cannot prove his innocence. The
instrusion of real love — finally consummated — for a time takes
Vol'skii's mind off his problem; he dreams of marrying Irina and
of living with her happily ever after. The awakening comes when
his closest friend tells Vol'skii that Chernov has carried out his
threat and has stamped him a denunciator. At work Vol'skii's

formerly friendly colleagues turn away from him. At home, his telephone keeps ringing, people renouncing their former friendship for him. His only hope in the terrifying vacuum that begins to surround him is Irina. But when she finally comes, he realizes that she too has left him — not because she believes in his guilt, but because she is unable to fight for a man thus stigmatized. Under the burden of complete isolation, Vol'skii's psyche gives way, and he ends up in an insane asylum.

The ideas which Arzhak incorporated in "Atonement" are many-fold, quite complex, and it is impossible to find one inter-pretation for the story. On the most obvious political level, "Atonement" reflects the feelings of guilt which haunt a whole generation for having suffered and condoned Stalin's terror out of fear for personal safety. As a boy, Vol'skii remembers "a triumphant demonstration on the occasion of the death sentence of the heroes of the trial of 1937 or 38",[341] and himself quoting a poetic line (to his parents) condemning those who laugh at the victim of the executioner. But life had subsequently taught him to be more cautious and circumspect. At the time of the action of the story, Vol'skii has erased the past from his memory and lives like everybody else. ". . . There was some special picquancy in the fact that a cozy chat about the 'Comédie Française' was interrupted by the melancholic swearing (mat) of a dying camp inmate (dokhodiaka), in the fact that some sharp guys from the philological faculty talked about the alliterations and assonances of the cursed (okaiannyi) genre. Ladies flushed from drinking ice-cold vodka pronounced with gusto: 'Hey, chief, you chief (nachal'nichek), let me go home . . .'"[342] A national tragedy involving millions of human lives had been reduced to an abstraction.

The fact that Vol'skii does not fight Chernov, and eventually lets himself be destroyed, points to the second, psychological idea in the story: the problem of guilt through omission rather than com-

mission. This is brought out already at the beginning of the story
(chapter 2) by the writer Igol'nikov (another spokesman for the
author) who says: "First I categorically state that each person has
harmed another one at least once in his life: you, and he, and
I. Second — and this is the most important thing — you are guilty
of what you have not done. Don't you feel that you are persecuted
by specters of things not done? Don't you dream at night of
embryos of actions, victims of abortions, actions which you
artificially aborted?"[343] But Igol'nikov is an exception rather than
the rule, and most other people surrounding Vol'skii are either
unaware or unwilling to recognize their guilts of omission, and
perhaps to suppress any personal qualms, gladly raise the first stone
against Vol'skii as soon as he is compromised. Again, as in "This Is
Moscow Speaking" the motif of cowardice, of a Pontius Pilate
washing his hands of responsibility and involvement, is sounded
by Arzhak. Lonely and desperate, Vol'skii hurls his accusation at
these people, including his former self:

"Long live the liberal intelligentsia! Long live the stern
guardians of morality! Long live our thinking (mysliashchaia)
youth! You are right, my friends . . . And I am right too . . . There
are two of us, Viktor Vol'skii. One of them is sitting here, in this
room, and takes a decision; the other of us sits there, at Lur'e's or at
Riazhentsev's, and speaks with indignation about the first one, the
scum, the denunciator. Put yourself in his place, Vol'skii number
one. Try, find at least some kind of justification for a denunciator
like yourself. There is no justification. You are doomed, number
one. Number two has sentenced you. And you, number two, the
judge, are also sentenced. We can now become united into one
whole and pay for ourselves and for all. For inaction, for that
which has not been done. Do you hear, admirers of Hemingway,
Picasso, and Prokof'ev, I will pay not for that guilt which you have

thought up, but for the one which really exists, for my guilt and yours! Yours! Yours!"[344]

Underlying the problem of guilt through omission lies a conscious non-involvement and separation from life which, Arzhak seems to say, leads to ruin. Like Kafka's hero in *The Trial* (although it is impossible to prove Arzhak's connection to Kafka, there are some Kafkaesque elements in the story) Vol'skii had led a completely self-centered, unthinking existence, and is therefore brought to trial. One cannot and must not be silent and inactive. "You must answer for yourself and by that you are answering for others" Anatolii Kartsev had said at the end of "This Is Moscow Speaking." After Irina who could have saved him by her love and loyalty, leaves him, Vol'skii finally realizes his "guilt", and accepts suffering. Here the Christian (and Dostoevskian) motif of suffering as an important ingredient of real life seems to come in. Vol'skii had shunned it as far as possible. But when Chernov realizes his threat, he for the first time in his life learns what it means to suffer. A fantastic dialogue with poster figures in Vol'skii's office externalizes the conflict in the hero's mind: "The main thing is that you know that you are not guilty," says one figure. "I know it, but does it make it easier for me?" Vol'skii retorts. "Who told you that one has to live always easily? It's enough if you have lived like that for 37 years." "But how am I to live among people?" Vol'skii asks. "Suffer," the poster figure tells him.[345]

Even if Vol'skii's last action — his frantic call for personal liberation from lies and oppression, made at the concert of an American Negro singer — or perhaps even his madness, make for his ultimate atonement, on the metaphysical level the question of good and evil seems to remain unresolved. In a symbolic authorial vision Arzhak presents Good and Evil engaged in a game of chess: "... Evil ... had no reason to hurry. It moved the pawns, strengthened its positions, unhurriedly developed its chessmen. The

bishops of Evil struck obliquely, impetuously like rapiers. With
fantastic, unnatural vagaries the knights of Evil jumped. With
clatter pawns rolled down into nowhere. Most often they were the
pawns of Good. It gladly sacrificed them in the hope of a quick
win. Evil spared its own . . . 'Well, let's have the last game', Good
would say after having just lost. And Evil always agreed . . .''[346]
In the final analysis Evil as such seems to keep the upper hand, with
Good fighting a hasty, impotent and futile battle against it.

      Even more than in "This Is Moscow Speaking" Arzhak's
characters in "Atonement" are psychological "types" rather than
individuals in their own right. Viktor Vol'skii is as already
mentioned, extremely close to Anatolii Kartsev (and ultimately to
the author himself), both in biographical data and attitudes. He is
again a middle-aged, intelligent *homo Sovieticus*, basically decent,
but a conformist out of necessity and fear. Still, like many of Tertz's
characters, Vol'skii too seems to suffer from a feeling of spiritual
(or even religious) emptiness, even if he tries to dismiss it. Looking
at the ruins of the church of Christ the Savior, destroyed by the
government in 1934, Vol'skii thinks: ". . . Of course, there can be
no doubt that there is no use in churches — they are architectural
monuments, not more, and still . . . They blew up God, and the
wave of explosion wounded man, gave him a shell-shock. Deafness,
dumbness . . . Pus is flowing from under the bandages, from under
the articles (stateiki) about humanism. Of course, the doctors say
'pus is flowing — the wound is clearing up.' Well, let's see."[347]
The moral dilemma which Vol'skii has to face is similar to
Kartsev's, and the path which he eventually follows is also the
same: an acceptance of responsibility, no matter what its consequences. Perhaps it is a sign of Arzhak's gradual disillusionment
with the world of reality that made him let Kartsev win, and
Vol'skii lose in the contest between good and evil, courage and

cowardice. Vol'skii's final words from the insane asylum have a deeply moving ring of desperation and pathos:

"Sometimes, when my head does not ache and there is no rain in the streets, I would like to go somewhere far, far where there are not so many people. They are all very clever and kind, but I am so tired, so tired because they are always with me. I very much want to be alone . . . I will wait for the winter when it will snow, or even better, for a snowstorm so that they could not find me by my footprints. I will wait for a stormy night, I will put on my dressing gown and will open the door with the triangular key which I found and hid in my underwear. By the way, this key looks like those keys which are used to open up railroad carriages. I will go away, and will again be alone . . ."[348]

A similarly schematic treatment is accorded to the other characters in the story. Irina, Vol'skii's beloved, is a typical young Soviet woman, talented and loving, who nevertheless proves too weak to fight against a prevalent opinion. Chernov who appears and disappears out of nowhere like a spirit of vengeance is only memorable through his impassionate outburst against Vol'skii which provides a glimpse into the horrors of concentration camps: "There, in the camp, I decided to kill you. I would kill you for my defiled (ispoganennaia) life, for the fact that we ate watery soup (balanda), for the fact that we slept with wet feet, for the fact that the Investigator spat in my face and I was not allowed to wipe off his spittle, for the fact that Liuda married another man — without love, crying — so that she, expelled everywhere could feed her child, my child, it was born after I was taken away . . ."[349] The most human character in the story is the writer Igol'nikov, a member of the Union of Soviet Writers, a "repenting intellectual" (kaiushchiisia intelligent) who is suffering from a feeling of guilt for inaction, for having become resigned in his official career, for following the principle of non-interference ("ne vredi"). He is the only person

who dares to come to Vol'skii after the latter has been ostracized
by everyone, who tries to cheer him up, and who spends an evening
drinking with him, and philosophizing upon the Russian national
character. It is interesting that Arzhak's Slavophile attitudes are
again very close to Tertz's: "... We Russians are good-natured
because of lack of will-power, because of a feeling of doom,
because everything around, everything that has been and is — are
optical illusions, phantoms. Everything is unstable and shaky. And
we are vicious for the same reason ... An American or a Swede ...
will not be good or bad for no reason. They have a concrete,
utilitarian conception about justice. They don't throw their
emotions around. They are economical in regard to themselves and
time. But we are stupidly proud of throwing not a minute, not 24
hours, not years, but a whole life, a whole epoch to the wind. We
know ourselves that we are fools, and yet we are proud of it ...
Heart-to-heart talk, Vitia, is such a currency for which you can't
buy a damn abroad. And we in Russia sit in dirt (der'mo) up to our
ears and carry on such heart-to-heart conversations ...".[350] And as
a counterpart to Igol'nikov, Arzhak presents the somber, terrifying
image of a retired KGB official, whom the drunken hero meets in a
restaurant, and who tells him of his hope for the restoration of the
good, old times of Stalin.

Despite a basic canvas of realistic description, "Atonement"
has an interesting super-structure of poetry, fantasy and symbolism.
The epigraph to the story — a poem by "Il'ia Chur" — echoes
Pushkin's motif of the eternal hostility between the poet and the
crowd, to which is added a modern touch: the willingness of the
common man to denounce those who are above him. A Gipsy song,
allegedly composed by one of the characters in the story (Misha
Lur'e), stresses the idea of freedom and joyful abandon which does
not exist in the reality which surrounds all characters. Finally,

another poem by a young, modern poet speaks of the belance of good and evil, light and darkness as the core of life.

The most interesting non-realistic devices in the story are the italicized authorial asides, which are inserted at crucial points in the narrative (chapters 4, 7, 10). The symbolic contest between Good and Evil in chapter 4 is followed by an aside in which the author tries to find a happy solution for his hero, but ends up with the words: "I cannot help you in any way. You are doomed, Viktor . . ."[351] The final aside, which implies Vol'skii's innocence (it transpires that it was Chernov's friend who had meanwhile committed suicide who had denounced him) is the most obscure of all. It is presented in the form of a dialogue between a person (the author?) and a powerful being who refuses to take any action: "Well, listen, you certainly know that I do not interfere in their affairs, I only evaluate them . . . Understand: everything follows its course . . . And in the final analysis, he is really guilty, if not of that, then something else . . . So what, if he is talented, what significance does it have . . . Of course, it is a pity . . . A great, great pity . . ."[352]

Finally, Vol'skii's dream in which he sees himself in a boat, rushing through stormy waves to perdition, and surrounded by people who cannot hear him, should be mentioned as another example of symbolism, foreshadowing the hero's ruin.

A deceptively simple, real-life plot — an unjust accusation of guilt — skillfully developed and raised to a profound metaphysical level, shows Arzhak's literary capacities at their best. It is regrettable that "Atonement" remained his last story, and tragic that he too had to atone for it with the best years of his life.

Footnotes

1. Cf. Boris Filippov's introduction to Arzhak's story. "This Is Moscow Speaking," printed in the Russian original ("Govorit Moskva"), Washington, 1962. Cited at the trial; see *Belaia kniga o dele Siniavskogo i Danielia (The White Book on the case of Siniavskii and Daniel')*, compiled by Aleksandr Gintsburg, Moscow 1966, printed by Posev, Frankfurt/Main, 1967, p. 190. Henceforth referred to as *Belaia kniga.*

2. *Belaia kniga,* pp. 305; 306. Italics of the original.

3. Many of the discussions of Tertz written primarily at the height of the political "case" were cursory, and often not only superficial but inaccurate. Among critics who used a more careful, literary approach to Tertz's works are Andrew Field (articles in "The New Leader" — May 13, 1963, July 19, 1965, November 8, 1965, February 14, 1966), and the introduction to the Russian edition of Tertz's *Thoughts Unaware (Mysli vrasplokh)*, Rausen Publishers, N. Y. 1966, and Mihajlo Mihajlov in his "Abram Tertz: Flight from the Testtube" in *Russian Themes*, Farrar, Straus, Giroux. N. Y. 1968. While the credit for "discovering" Tertz for the English-speaking public belongs to Mr. Field, I cannot agree with his excessively psycho-pathological, Freudian approach, which has little basis in the actual text. I likewise cannot accept Mr. Mihajlov's strongly religious-philosophical interpretation of Tertz's stories, "The Trial Begins," "You and I" and "The Icicle."

4. Quoted by Hélène Peltier-Zamoiska in her article on Siniavskii in "Le Monde," April 17, 1966, cf. *Belaia kniga,* p. 281. Hélène Peltier-Zamoiska, daughter of a French naval attaché in Moscow, attended Moscow University as a student of Russian literature after the end of World War II, where she met Siniavskii.

5. "Inostrannaia literatura," ("Foreign Literature"), 1962, No. 1

6. The actual arrests took place earlier: Siniavskii was arrested on September 8, 1965, in the street, while on his way to deliver his first lecture at the Theater School named after Nemirovich-Danchenko; Daniel' was arrested on September 12, 1965, while leaving

Vnukovo airport upon arrival from Novosibirsk, cf. *Belaia kniga,*
p. 9

7. January 13, 1966

8. "Nasledniki Smerdiakova," ("The Heirs of Smerdiakov"), in "Li-
    teraturnaia gazeta" ("Literary Gazette"), January 22, 1966; cf.
    also *Belaia kniga,* pp. 107—116

9. For a full account of the trial in English, see *On Trial, The Soviet
    State Versus "Abram Tertz" and "Nikolai Arzhak,"* translated,
    edited and with an introduction by Max Hayward, Harper and
    Row, N. Y. 1966. In Russian, see *Belaia kniga,* pp. 167—327

10. It was thanks to Gintsburg's remarkable painstaking work and his
    courage that we dispose of most of the material in the Siniavskii-
    Daniel' case, which would otherwise have been hushed up and
    remained unknown. Gintsburg was tried and sentenced together
    with three friends (Iurii Galanskov, Aleksei Dobrovol'skii and
    Vera Lashkova) for work on "underground" poetry collections
    ("Phoenix" and "Syntax"), as well as the compilation of *The
    White Book,* the latter being probably the heavier "crime." It
    seems that he was sent to the same labor camp (Potma, 17. Lag-
    punkt, Mordvinian SSR) where Daniel' was being kept, and that
    they met there. Incidentally, Daniel''s wife, Larisa Bogoraz-Bukh-
    man who participated in a sit-in demonstration against the invasion
    of Czechoslovakia in Moscow's Red Square in August 1968, has
    been tried and sent to a labor camp in Siberia (lumber-cutting and
    working shop in Chunia, Irkutsk area), cf. "Posev," August, 1969

11. cf. "Le Monde", April 17, 1966; also *Belaia kniga,* p. 280

12. *Belaia kniga,* p. 281

13. *ibid.,* p. 280

14. "Le Monde,", November 23, 1965; cf. also *Belaia kniga,* p. 30

15. Svetlana Allilueva, *Tol'ko odin god (Only One Year),* Harper and
    Row, N. Y., 1969, p. 243

16. *ibid.,* p. 244

17. "Vestnik Moskovskogo Universiteta", ("The Messenger of Moscow
    University"), 1950, vol. 1

18. Siniavskii is mentioned as one of the contributors in *Ocherk istorii russkoi sovetskoi literatury*, Akademiia Nauk SSSR, Moscow, 1955, part 2 (1935—54), and in *Russkaia sovetskaia literatura. Ocherk istorii (1917—46)*, Institut mirovoi literatury im. M. A. Gor'kogo, M. 1963. Cf. also his articles on the artistic structure of Gor'kii's novel *The Life of Klim Samgin* ("O khudozhestvennoi strukture romana *Zhizn' Klima Samgina*"), in *Tvorchestvo Maksima Gor'kogo i voprosy sotsialisticheskogo realizma.* Akademiia Nauk SSSR, M. 1958, pp. 132—174; cf. his articles on Gor'kii and Bagritskii, "A. M. Gor'kii", "Eduard Bagritskii", in vol. 1 of the 3 volume edition of *Istoriia russkoi sovetskoi literatury*, Akademiia Nauk SSSR, Institut Mirovoi literatury, M. 1958, pp. 99—167, and 397—420; cf. his article on Gor'kii as satirist ("Gor'kii kak satirik") in *O khudozhestvennom masterstve M. Gor'kogo,* Akademiia Nauk SSSR, M. 1960, pp. 131—173

19. For reasons unclear to a Western observer, Siniavskii's and Menshutin's names are nowhere mentioned in the anthology. They are, however, named as editors of it in a review of the anthology in "Novyi Mir", (No. 2, 1959, pp. 211—266), the author of which is dissatisfied with the selection of poetry made, and with its allegedly low artistic merit.

20. B. Pasternak, *Stikhi i poemy,* Bol'shaia biblioteka poeta, M. 1965

21. "Znanie" Publishing house, Moscow

22. Another unpublished piece of writing which was confiscated at the time was entitled "Tochka otscheta" (opyt samoanaliza) — cf. *Belaia kniga,* p. 238

23. Siniavskii's review of Evtushenko's poem "The Bratsk Hydroelectric station" ("Bratskaia GEZ"), was available only in an English translation which appeared in "Encounter", April 1967

24. *Belaia kniga,* p. 241. As in the case of the biographical data, our information here is, unfortunately, not complete.

25. Much has been made of the fact that Siniavskii, a Russian, chose a Jewish pseudonym while Daniel', a Jew, chose a non-Jewish one. This lead, among other things, to accusations of "anti-Semitism" against Siniavskii at the trial. However, this is completely unjusti-

fied. Both in Siniavskii's and Daniel"'s stories there are remarks by various characters that are sometimes hostile to Jews. This seems to reflect the attitude of certain parts of the population today, and is nothing else but a strain of "realism" in their not always realistic tales. In the case of Tertz, furthermore, it may be an intentional playing with a "tabu" subject, while his name may reflect his love for mystification.

26. There are, most probably, autobiographical elements in the description of the ideological conflict between "fathers" and "sons" in "The Trial Begins"

27. "Chto takoe sotsialisticheskii realizm?" ("What Is Socialist Realism?"), in *Fantasticheskii mir Abrama Tertsa (The Fantastic World of Abram Tertz)*, Inter-Language Literary Associates, N. Y. 1967, p. 444. All quotations are from this Russian edition of Tertz's work, which will be henceforth referred to as *Fantasticheskii mir.*

28. "O khudozhestvennoi strukture romana *Zhizn' Klima Samgina*, in *Tvorchestvo M. Gor'kogo i voprosy sotsialisticheskogo realizma*, Akademiia Nauk SSSR, M, 1958, pp. 132—174

29. "Mnogogolosie": ". . . a conversation is carried on by many characters at the same time and assumes such as quick and chaotic nature that the author puts down only separate remarks or parts of remarks leaving out all other connecting links." *In ibid.*

30. The reference is to Lev Tikhomirov (1850—1923), a member of the executive committee of the revolutionary People's Will (Narodnaia Volia) who was active in preparing the assassination of Czar Alexander II, and who later repented. Gor'kii, *Collected Works (Sobranie Sochinenii v 30 tomakh*, M., 1950), vol. 18, p. 424

31. "Novyi Mir," 1960, No. 5, pp. 225—236

32. "Novyi Mir," 1964, No. 1, pp. 260—263

33. "Novyi Mir," 1959, No. 8, pp. 248—254

34. *Belaia* kniga, pp. 144—145

35. The Russian title has been translated by George Dennis as "On Socialist Realism" (Pantheon Books. N. Y. 1960), which does not do justice to the Russian original and its obvious allusion to the whole tradition of 19th century polemical writings, especially

Tolstoi. The date of writing of this essay is not quite clear. Siniavskii at his trial stated that he had written it in 1958. (Cf. *Belaia kniga*, p. 204.) In Hayward's translation of the trial, the date is given as 1956 (*On Trial*, p. 88).
36. *Fantasticheskii mir*, pp. 412—413
37. *ibid.*, p. 417
38. *ibid.*, p. 431
39. *ibid.*, p. 440
40. *ibid.*, p. 440
41. Byt is a virtually untranslatable word which implies the totality of mores, habits, thoughts of people of any given social class.
42. *Fantasticheskii, mir*, p. 444
43. *ibid.*, p. 446
44. It is, of course, impossible to ascertain whether these similarities are accidental or not, even if it can be assumed that Tertz was familiar with Tolstoi's essay.
45. Tertz is primarily concerned with the *literary* aspect of socialist realism, and seems to disregard intentionally the basic dialectical contradiction which is inherent in the concept. In his review of Tertz's essay Gleb Zekulin points out that Marxist philosophy sees tension (between the claims of literature and those of politics) as unavoidable. At any given time one of the contradictions must be predominant, and in the official view of socialist realism the predominant side is the political one. "Soviet Studies", 1960, No. 4, pp. 432—541
46. *Fantasticheskii mir*, p. 442
47. *ibid.*, p. 422
48. *ibid.*, p. 416
49. *ibid.*, p. 424
50. *ibid.*, p. 406
51. *ibid.*, p. 445
52. F. Dostoevskii. *Zapiski iz podpol'ia (Notes from Underground)*, in *Sobranie sochinenu v 10 tomakh*, M. 1956, vol 4, p. 160
53. *Fantasticheskii, mir*, p. 436
54. *ibid.*, p. 406

55. *ibid.*, p. 405
56. *ibid.*, p. 420
57. Dostoevskii, *Zapiski iz podpol'ia*, p. 152
58. Dostoevskii, *Besy (The Possessed)*, YMCA Press, Paris, vol. 1, p. 427
59. *Fantasticheskii* mir, p. 411
60. It is interesting that this issue seems to have bothered Tertz for some time. Hélène Peltier-Zamoiska mentions in her article that one of her first topics of conversation with Siniavskii was the question about "the choice which Ivan Karamazov had: whether one could build a crystal palace on the corpse of a child." "Le Monde," April 17, 18, 1966, quoted in *Belaia, kniga*, p. 281
61. *Fantasticheskii mir*, p. 436
62. The Russian term "Sud idet" may also mean "The Court is in Session," in judicial terminology.
63. Siniavskii himself insisted at the trial, that the story was "an artistic work, not a political document," cf. *Belaia kniga*, p. 225
64. *Fantasticheskii mir*, p. 233
65. Only the epilogue takes place in Siberia and is dated 1956
66. In his introduction to the Russian edition of *Thoughts Unaware (Mysli vrasplokh)* Andrew Field points to Andrei Belyi's novel as one of the "fictional forebears" of Tertz's story. *Thoughts Unaware*, Rausen Publishers and Distributors, N. Y., 1966, pp. 21, 22
67. *Fantasticheskii mir*, p. 258
68. *ibid.*, pp. 267, 268
69. *ibid.*, pp. 230—231
70. *ibid.*, p. 267
71. *ibid.*, p. 230
72. *ibid.*, p. 201
73. *ibid.*, p. 205
74. *ibid.*, pp. 207—208
75. *ibid.*, pp. 209—210
76. *ibid.*, pp. 210—211
77. *ibid.*, p. 234
78. *ibid.*, p. 237
79. *ibid.*, p. 273

80. The threefold division of the main characters in the story is some-what reminiscent of a similar division in Olesha's novel *Envy*, where Ivan Babichev and Kavalerov stand for the past, Andrei Babichev for the present, and Volodia Makarov and Valia for the future. However, the whole problem in Olesha is symbolical-aesthetic rather than ideological-philosophical as it is in Tertz.

81. *Fantasticheskii mir*, p. 218
82. *ibid.*, p. 215
83. *ibid.*, p. 245
84. *ibid.*, p. 236
85. *ibid.*, p. 269
86. *ibid.*, p. 211
87. *ibid.*, p. 212
88. *ibid.*, p. 241
89. *ibid.*, p. 242
90. *ibid.*, p. 242
91. *ibid.*, p. 242
92. *ibid.*, p. 275
93. *ibid.*, p. 199
94. *ibid.*, pp. 200, 201
95. *ibid.*, p. 272
96. *ibid.*, p. 220
97. *ibid.*, p. 255
98. *ibid.*, pp. 268—269
99. *ibid.*, pp. 250, 251; the third and fourth words from the end are untranslatable endings of Russian *abstracta*.
100. "Pkhents" cannot be accurately dated, since it appeared in the West (in the journal "Encounter," April 1966) after Siniavskii's trial and sentencing.
101. *Fantasticheskii mir*, p. 423
102. *ibid.*, pp. 32, 33
103. *ibid.*, p. 34
104. *Mysli vrasplokh (Thoughts Unaware)*, Rausen Publishers, N. Y. 1966, p. 79; italics mine.
105. *ibid.*, pp. 79—80

106. There is a kind of inversion of Gogolian fantasy, for the fantastic trick is completely explainable in terms of mass hypnotism.
107. *Fantasticheskii mir*, pp. 27–28
108. *ibid.*, p. 29
109. *ibid.*, p. 31
110. *ibid.*, pp. 39–40
111. *ibid.*, p. 41
112. A stylized imitation of the speech of a person from a special (usually low) social stratum, prominently used in Russian literature since e.g. Nikolai Leskov.
113. Tertz, it must be noted, is not completely consistent in his use of one narrative voice (cf. his later stories). He does switch occasionally from the 3rd person narrative to the 1st person (perhaps, Kostia's thoughts during the first theft) or to the 2nd person (again Kostia, or a generalized narrator, who could be even the author himself).
114. *Fantasticheskii mir*, p. 32
115. *ibid.*, p. 32
116. *ibid.*, p. 33
117. *ibid.*, p. 104
118. *ibid.*, p. 85
119. *ibid.*, p. 77. Tertz is apparently parodying here Chekhov's playwright Trigorin in *The Seagull*, or Vera Iosifovna in "Ionych," cf. *Polnoe Sobranie sochinenii*, M. 1948, vol. XI, p. 166 and vol IX, p. 286 sq
120. *Fantasticheskii mir*, p. 82
121. *ibid.*, p. 89
122. *ibid.*, p. 90
123. *ibid.*, p. 101
124. *ibid.*, p. 101
125. *ibid.*, p. 88
126. *ibid.*, pp. 95–96
127. *ibid.*, p. 94
128. *ibid.*, p. 80
129. *ibid.*, p. 97
130. *ibid.*, p. 97

131. *ibid.*, p. 107
132. Cf. Straustin's literary method mentioned above.
133. *ibid.*, pp. 97—98. The digression on cucumbers and on Russia are strongly suggestive of a take-off on Gogol's famous digressions, especially in *Dead Souls.*
134. *ibid.*, p. 105
135. Siniavskii's wife who protested the arrest of her husband in a letter to Brezhnev and other high Party officials (December 24, 1965) attached to it a copy of "The Tenants" with the following comment: "Those of you who live in communal apartments, will understand whether this story is slanderous, anti-Soviet. (I, however, have been living in such conditions for 35 years, and Siniavskii for 40)." *Belaia kniga*, pp. 65—66
136. The name is derived from the dialectal word "anchutka" 'devil,' used in the Riazan' area.
137. *Fantasticheskii* mir, p. 70
138. *ibid.*, pp. 73—74
139. *ibid.*, p. 67
140. *ibid.*, p. 71
141. *ibid.*, p. 68
142. *ibid.*, p. 68
143. *ibid.*, p. 69
144. *ibid.*, p. 72
145. *ibid.*, p. 76
146. *ibid.*, p. 49
147. A. Field, Introduction to *Thoughts Unaware*, p. 11
148. *Fantasticheskii mir*, p. 43
149. *ibid.*, p. 43
150. Again, an echo of Gogol in "Nevskii Prospekt," cf. the adventures of Pirogov and Piskarev with their respective beauties or "Povest' o tom kak possorilsia Ivan Ivanovich s Ivanom Nikiforovichem," where not "our Ivan Ivanovich but another one" is being mentioned.
151. *Fantasticheskii mir*, p. 47
152. *ibid.*, p. 45
153. *ibid.*, p. 60

154. *ibid.*, p. 62
155. *ibid.*, p. 62
156. Field, Introduction to *Thoughts Unaware*, pp. 11, 12. While the homosexual element escapes me entirely, the morbid eroticism which is rather obvious (cf. especially the final scene between Lida and Ippolit) is rather typical for Tertz's general negative attitude toward sex ("black magic").
157. M. Mihajlov, "Abram Tertz: Flight from the Testtube," p. 15
158. *Fantasticheskii mir*, p. 53
159. *ibid.*, p. 46
160. *ibid.*, p. 47
161. The Russian title "Gololeditsa" means "ice-covered [slippery] ground"
162. The exact details of Natasha's death are revealed to the hero actually after the New Year's party.
163. *ibid.*, pp. 112—113. A similar transformation, altough reversed, from fantasy to reality, occurs at the moment of Natasha's death, when the hero loses his clairvoyance, and when the formerly luxurious prison is suddenly seen by him as primitive, dirty, unattractive, while colonel Tarasov loses his former radiance and firmness, and fades into an old, tired, wrinkled man.
164. The fact that the ballerina had lost one of her legs in an accident and is wearing an artificial aluminum limb, made for her in Berlin 30 years earlier, at the expense of her former admirer, admiral Kurbatov, has a Gogolian touch, both in the superfluity and grotesqueness of this information, for the ballerina never reappears in the story.
165. *Fantasticheskii mir*, pp. 120—121
166. *ibid.*, p. 122
167. *ibid.*, p. 123
168. *ibid.*, p. 124
169. *ibid.*, p. 131
170. *ibid.*, p. 132
171. *ibid.*, p. 133
172. *ibid.*, p. 149

173. *ibid.*, p. 118
174. *ibid.*, p. 125
175. Cf. similar reflections on the theory of evolution by Karlinskii in "The Trial Begins".
176. *ibid.*, p. 142
177. *ibid.*, p. 143
178. *ibid.*, p. 125
179. *ibid.*, p. 124
180. *ibid.*, p. 157
181. *ibid.*, p. 174
182. *ibid.*, p. 170
183. *ibid.*, p. 174
184. *ibid.*, p. 140
185. *ibid.*, p. 108
186. *ibid.*, p. 156
187. *ibid.*, p. 129
188. *ibid.*, p. 130
189. *ibid.*, pp. 165—166
190. Tertz's familiarity with H. G. Wells had been pointed out in "The Trial Begins." In "Pkhents" there is likewise a reference to Wells' *War of the Worlds*, p. 187
191. *Fantasticheskii mir*, p. 187
192. *ibid.*, p. 195
193. *ibid.*, p. 177
194. *ibid.*, p. 175
195. *ibid.*, pp. 179—180
196. Cf. the same motif in "The Icicle," in the narrator's encounter with his pre-historic ancestor.
197. *ibid.*, p. 181
198. *ibid.*, p. 191
199. *ibid.*, p. 188
200. *ibid.*, p. 188
201. *ibid.*, p. 194
202. *ibid.*, p. 195; it is possible that these words have a meaning, but can be de-coded only by the author himself.

203. *ibid.*, pp. 192—193
204. *ibid.*, pp. 185—186
205. The English rendition of *Liubimov* as *The Makepeace Experiment* (Pantheon Books, N. Y., 1965) is derived from an inexact translation of the name of its hero, Tikhomirov [quiet, gentle + peace, world]. The name is so common in Russian, however, that it has lost much of its original, etymological meaning. The title *Liubimov* could be more precisely rendered as *The Beloved Town*.
206. At his trial, Siniavskii termed it "a lyrical work," *Belaia kniga*, p. 229
207. *Fantasticheskii mir*, p. 300
208. *ibid., p.* 324
209. This episode is strongly suggestive of the campaign of mayor Borodavkin against the settlement of Negodnitsa, during which his "army" gets lost in the middle of the day, while being virtually there. Cf. Saltykov-Shchedrin, *Istoriia odnogo goroda.*
210. His letter to his friend Tolia (who also appeared in "The Trial Begins") in chapter 6 in which he shows clearly that he has been successfully brainwashed by Lenia, shows him as a staunch, blind instrument of whatever ideology (or Purpose) happens to dominate at the moment.
211. *Fantasticheskii mir*, p. 287
212. *ibid.*, p. 288
213. *ibid.*, p. 289. An allusion to the ending of Pushkin's *Boris Godunov*.
214. *Fantasticheskii mir*, p. 289
215. *ibid.*, p. 290
216. *ibid.*, p. 312
217. *ibid.*, pp. 315, 316. It had been mentioned earlier by the narrator that Mariamov had lost his arm after having assisted in the demolition of a monastery in Liubimov, known for its miraculous healings, in the 1920's — the "period of struggle with illiteracy." While the four other participants in that action died, "accidentally, within a short period of time", Mariamov's hand withered and became useless.
218. *Fantasticheskii mir*, p. 314; italics of the original.

219. *ibid.,* p. 317
220. *ibid.,* p. 344
221. Introduction to the Russian language edition of *Liubimov,* Washington, 1964, p. 11
222. Introduction to *Thoughts Unaware,* pp. 26, 27
223. At the trial Siniavskii disclaimed the comparisons made between Saltykov's "History" of the town "Glupov" and that of his own "Liubimov" on the basis of his own (positive) and Saltykov-Shchedrin's (negative) attitudes toward their respective topics. *Belaia kniga,* p. 229
224. In her Tranlator's Notes, of the English edition of *Liubimov (The Makepeace Experiment,* Pantheon Books, N. Y. 1965) Manya Harari connects Lenia with Lenin, with len' (idleness), leshii (woodspirit), Khrushchev, and Stalin!
225. It is, of course, impossible to ascertain whether Tertz knew this particular story by Wells, or whether he accidentally hit on a similar theme. However, certain parallels between the two stories are rather striking: While at first Fartheringay limits himself to small feats like wishing for a new toothbrush, and 3 eggs for breakfast (Lenia's first trick, incidentally, is to turn Savelii Kuzmich upside down on the floor), soon, with the help of Pastor Maydig, he goes over to "doing good" and improving the world: thus they reform the pastor's drunkard housekeeper (who suddenly smashes her private bottle of brandy), then take on other alcoholics, changing their beer and liquor to water, try to improve communication, drawn out a swamp, etc. It is only when Pastor Maydig suggests to George Fartheringay that he stop the rotation of the globe that the catastrophe occurs: all movable objects (including the two protagonists) fly through the air, the hero wishes to renounce his miraculous abilities, and when he recovers his senses, he finds himself in the same tavern where he performed his first miracle — without memory of the past, or any miraculous powers.
226. *Fantasticheskii mir,* pp. 328—329. Tertz is fond of quoting (ironically) one of Gor'kiis favorite maxims.

227. *ibid.*, p. 337. A similar scene occurs in Saltykov-Shchedrin's *History of a Town*, where its mayor, Ugrium-Burcheev (satire on Arakcheev) orders everyone to work upon his commando.
228. *ibid.*, p. 340
229. *ibid.*, p. 323
230. *ibid.*, p. 346
231. *ibid., p. 346.* In Saltykov-Shchedrin's novel mayor Ugrium-Burcheev wants similarly to rename Glupov into Nepreklonsk.
232. *ibid.*, pp. 296; 297
233. *ibid.*, p. 329
234. *ibid.*, p. 319
235. *ibid.*, p. 387
236. *ibid.*, p. 332
237. *ibid.*, p. 282
238. *ibid.*, p. 333
239. *ibid.*, p. 318
240. *ibid.*, p. 349
241. *ibid.*, p. 394
242. *ibid.*, p. 311
243. *ibid.*, pp. 279; 281
244. *ibid.*, p. 282
245. *ibid.*, p. 385
246. *ibid.*, p. 308
247. *ibid.*, p. 283
248. *ibid.*, p. 284
249. *ibid.*, pp. 396—397
250. *ibid.*, p. 280
251. *ibid.*, p. 380
252. *ibid.*, p. 362
253. *ibid.*, p. 363
254. *ibid.*, p. 334
255. *ibid.*, p. 336
256. *ibid.*, p. 338
257. *ibid.*, p. 291
258. *ibid.*, p. 383

259. *ibid.*, p. 310
260. *ibid.*, p. 371
261. *ibid.*, p. 364
262. *ibid.*, pp. 367—368
263. The translation of the title as "Thoughts at Random" or "Thoughts Unaware" does not convey the exact meaning in Russian, which is rather "Thoughts caught off-guard." The date of writing is not exactly known, but must be before 1963, the date when Tertz sent them abroad. Cf. *Belaia kniga,* p. 205
264. Especially his late writings such as *Uedinennoe,* 1912 and *Opavshie list'ia,* 1912, 1913
265. Thus Iurii Ivask, in V. V. Rozanov. *Izbrannoe,* Chekhov Publishing house, N. Y. 1956, p. 10
266. e.g. Rozanov: "... the feeling for God is the most transcendental [feeling] in man," p. 66 in the above edition; "The most dangerous aspect of Christianity in the 19th century is the fact that it is becoming rhetorical," *ibid.,* p. 69: "Death ... is the tragedy of tragedies," *ibid.,* p. 107: "I could renouce gifts,literature, the future of my I, glory or fame ... but I could never renounce God, *ibid.,* p. 212
267. *Mysli vrasplokh,* Rausen Publishers. N. Y. 1966, p. 117. All subsequent quotes refer to this edition.
268. *ibid.*, p. 119
269. *ibid.*, p. 64
270. *ibid.*, p. 66
271. *ibid.*, p. 48
272. *ibid.*, pp. 59—60
273. *ibid.*, p. 68
274. *ibid.*, p. 133
275. *ibid.*, p. 133
276. *ibid.*, p. 134
277. *ibid.*, p. 92
278. *ibid.*, p. 122
279. *ibid.*, p. 132
280. *ibid.*, pp. 120—121

281. *ibid.*, p. 50
282. *ibid.*, p. 110
283. *ibid.*, p. 121
284. *ibid.*, p. 86
285. *ibid.*, p. 126
286. *ibid.*, p. 127
287. *ibid.*, p. 140
288. *ibid.*, p. 141
289. *ibid.*, p. 137
290. *ibid.*, pp. 138—139
291. *ibid.*, p. 84
292. *ibid.*, pp. 79—80
293. *ibid.*, p. 47
294. *ibid.*, p. 131
295. *ibid.*, p. 72
296. *ibid.*, p. 46
297. *ibid.*, p. 129
298. *ibid.*, p. 97
299. *ibid.*, p. 130
300. *ibid.*, pp. 128—129; italics of the original.
301. *ibid.*, p. 107
302. *Belaia kniga*, pp. 147—148
303. *ibid.*, p. 194
304. Nikolai Arzhak, "Ruki," Washington, 1963, p. 7
305. *ibid.*, p. 9
306. *ibid.*, p. 9
307. *ibid.*, p. 10
308. *ibid.*, p. 11
309. *ibid.*, p. 8
310. *ibid.*, p. 8
311. *ibid.*, p. 9
312. *ibid.*, p. 11
313. The idea for the story was, incidentally, suggested to Arzhak by
     an acquaintance, Sergei Grigor'evich Khmel'nitskii, an architect
     who managed to whitewash himself completely at the trial. It is

also an interesting point in this connection that the theme of Arzhak's last story, "Atonement," bears a striking parallel to an episode from Khmel'nitskii's past. According to the information collected in *Belaia kniga*, Khmel'nitskii in 1963 was confronted by two former friends who accused him of having denounced them to the secret police in 1949, as a result of which they had been tried and sentenced. Khmel'nitskii who had just defended his doctoral dissertation is supposed to have left Moscow soon after that incident. Cf. *Belaia kniga*, pp. 262—263

314. *Belaia kniga*, p. 181
315. Nikolai Arzhak, "Govorit Moskva," Washington, 1962, pp. 12—13
316. Rumors and retrospective reminiscences about "the Day" by the other characters (chapter 8) gives a wider picture of what allegedly happened — squaring of political accounts in the Ukraine, national hostilities in the Caucasus, a boycott of the ordinance in the Baltic states, numerous victims in the RSFSR, cf. pp. 57—58
317. "Govorit Moskva," p. 16
318. *ibid.*, pp. 16—17
319. *ibid.*, p. 42
320. *ibid.*, p. 20
321. *ibid.*, p. 25
322. *ibid.*, pp. 43—44
323. *ibid.*, p. 45
324. *ibid.*, p. 61
325. *ibid.*, p. 18
326. *ibid.*, pp. 46—47
327. *ibid.*, pp. 22—23
328. *ibid.*, p. 17
329. *ibid.*, p. 28
330. *ibid.*, p. 40
331. At the trial Daniel said about the story: ". . . Why did I write it? Among my friends there are many scholars, and one of them told me about the ballyhoo raised around Bashian and Lepeshinskaia (I do not equate these two names), he told me, that the sensational news were harmful to our science. It was in connection with this

ballyhoo, and not in connection with science that the story was written . . ."
Belaia kniga, p. 195

332. Nikolai Arzhak, "Chelovek iz MINAPa," Washington, 1963, p. 18
333. *ibid.,* p. 17
334. *ibid.,* p. 24
335. *ibid.,* p. 26
336. *ibid.,* p. 28
337. *ibid.,* p. 31
338. *ibid.,* p. 36
339. There are actually only 11 chapters, chapter 4 being missing.
340. Nikolai Arzhak, "Iskuplenie", Inter Language Literary Associates, N. Y. 1964, p. 39
341. *ibid.,* p. 27
342. *ibid.,* p. 11
343. *ibid.,* p. 24
344. *ibid.,* p. 66
345. *ibid.,* pp. 34—35
346. *ibid.,* pp. 32—33
347. *ibid.,* p. 18
348. *ibid.,* p. 71
349. *ibid.,* p. 30
350. *ibid.,* pp. 63—64
351. *ibid.,* p. 55
352. *ibid.,* pp. 66; 67

Bibliography

I. Primary Sources (in Russian)

Tertz, Abram: *Fantasticheskii mir Abrama Tertsa.* Inter-Language Literary Associates, N. Y. 1967

— *Mysli vrasplokh.* Rausen Publishers, N. Y. 1966

Siniavskii, Andrei: "Ob estetike Maiakovskogo." *Vestnik Moskovskogo Universiteta,* No. 1, 1950

— "O khudozhestvennoi strukture romana Zhizn' Klima Samgina," in *Tvorchestvo Maksima Gor'kogo i voprosy sotsialisticheskogo realizma,* Akademiia Nauk SSSR, M. 1958, pp. 132–174

— "A. M. Gor'kii," in *Istoriia russkoi sovetskoi literatury,* Akademiia Nauk SSSR, Institut mirovoi literatury, M. 1958, vol. 1, pp. 99–167

— "O khudezhestvennom masterstve Maksima Gor'kogo," Akademiia Nauk SSSR, M. 1960, pp. 131–173

— "Eduard Bagritskii," in *Istoriia russkoi sovetskoi literatury,* Akademiia Nauk SSSR, Institut mirovoi literatury, M. 1958, vol. 1, pp. 397–420

— (contributor): in *Ocherk istorii russkoi sovetskoi literatury,* Akademiia Nauk SSSR, M. 1955, part 2 (1935–1954)

— (contributor): in *Russkaia sovetskaia literatura, Ocherk istorii (1917–1946),* Institut mirovoi literatury, M. 1963

Siniavskii, Andrei, and A. N. Menshutin: *Poeziia pervykh let revoliutsii, 1917–1920,* M. 1964

— *Den' russkoi poezii,* M. 1958

Siniavskii, Andrei, and I. N. Golomshtok: *Picasso* (?), Znanie, M. 1960

— Introduction to B. Pasternak, *Stikhotvoreniia i poemy,* M. 1961

— Introduction to B. Pasternak, *Stikhi i poemy,* M. 1965

— Review (Anatolii Safronov: "Ot vsekh shirot" Stikhi, Molodaia gvardiia, M. 1958), in *Novyi Mir,* August 1959, pp. 248–254

— Review ("Poeziia i proza Ol'gi Berggol'ts"), *Novyi Mir,* 1960, No. 5, pp. 225–236

— Review ("Poidem so mnoi", Robert Frost, Iz deviati knig, Translated and edited by M. A. Zenkevich, M. 1963), *Novyi Mir,* January 1964, pp. 260–263

Siniavskii, Andrei: Review (novel by Ivan Shevtsov, *Tlia*, M. 1964), *Novyi Mir*, 1964, No. 12, pp. 228–233
— Review (Evgenii Dolmatovskii, "Stikhi o nas," M. 1964), *Novyi Mir*, March 1965, pp. 244–248
— Review ("On Yevtuschenko"), *Encounter*, April 1967
Arzhak, Nikolai: "Govorit Moskva" (published by B. Filippov), Washington 1962
— "Ruki," "Chelovek iz MINAPa" (published by B. Filippov), Washington 1963
— "Iskuplenie." Inter-Language Literary Associates, N. Y. 1964
English translations
Tertz, Abram: *Fantastic Stories*. Pantheon Books, N. Y. 1963
— *On Socialist Realism*. Pantheon Books, N. Y. 1960
— *The Trial Begins*. Collins and Harvill, London 1960
— *The Makepeace Experiment*. Pantheon Books, N. Y. 1965
— "Thoughts Unaware." *New Leader*, July 19, 1965
Siniavskii, Andrei: *For Freedom of Imagination*. Holt, Rinehart, Winston, N. Y. 1971
Arzhak, Nikolai: *This Is Moscow Speaking and Other Stories*. Collins and Harvill, London 1968
II. Secondary Sources
Gintsburg, A. (editor, Moscow): *Belaia kniga po delu A. Siniavskogo i Iu. Danielia*. Published by Posev, Frankfurt/Main 1967
Hayward, Max (editor and translator): *On Trial: the Soviet State Versus "Abram Tertz" and "Nikolai Arzhak."* Harper and Row, N. Y. 1966
Field, A.: "Socialist Surrealism," *New Leader*, May 13, 1963
— "Abram Tertz's Ordeal by Mirror," *New Leader*, July 19, 1965
— "The Arrest of Andrei Siniavskii," *New Leader*, Nov. 8, 1965
— "Prisoner in Fantasy," *New Leader*, February 14, 1966
— Introduction to *Thoughts Unaware*. Rausen Publishers, N. Y. 1966
Mihajlov, Mihajlo: "Abram Tertz: Flight from the Testtube." In *Russian Themes*. Farrar, Straus, Giroux, N. Y. 1968
Allilueva, Svetlana: *Tol'ko odin god*. Harper and Row, N. Y. 1969